American Government

An Introduction Using MicroCase

Third Edition

MicroCase Corporation
Bellevue, Washington

AMERICAN GOVERNMENT: An Introduction Using MicroCase is published by MicroCase Corporation.

Series Editor	Rodney Stark
Acquisitions Editor	David Smetters
Editorial Assistant	R. K. Clancy
Production Supervisor	Jodi B. Gleason
Layout/Electronic Production	Michael Brugman Design
Copy Editor	Margaret Moore
Map and Graphics Editor	June B. Tandy

© 1995 by MicroCase Corporation. All rights reserved.

No part of this book may be reproduced, stored in a retrieval system, or transcribed, in any form or by any means, electronic, mechanical, photocopying, recording, or otherwise, without the prior written permission of the publisher, MicroCase Corporation, 1301 120th Avenue N.E., Bellevue, WA 98005, (206) 635-0293.

IBM PC and IBM PC DOS are registered trademarks of International Business Machines, Inc.
ShowCase and **MicroCase** are registered trademarks of MicroCase Corporation.

Printed in the United States of America
 3 4 5 6 7 8 9 10—97 96

CONTENTS

Preface v
Disclaimer of Warranty vi
Acknowledgements vii

Introduction

EXERCISE 1 Getting Started: Aspects of Federalism 1

PART I Voters and Elections

EXERCISE 2 Electoral and Popular Votes for President..13
EXERCISE 3 Voter Participation 21
EXERCISE 4 Exploring Election Polls: Who Votes? 31
EXERCISE 5 Who Votes for Whom? 43
EXERCISE 6 Elections and the Media 51

PART II Parties and Issues

EXERCISE 7   Party Preference and Political Labels...61
EXERCISE 8   The Tax Issue 71
EXERCISE 9   The Issue of Entitlements 77
EXERCISE 10 The Abortion Issue 85

PART III Institutions of Government

EXERCISE 11 Who's in the House and Senate? 93
EXERCISE 12 Congressional Parties and the Contract with America....................101
EXERCISE 13 Congressional Campaign Finances 111
EXERCISE 14 A Female or African-American President..117
EXERCISE 15 Confidence in Government 125

PART IV Freedom

EXERCISE 16 Civil Liberties: Free Speech..133
EXERCISE 17 Civil Rights: Segregation 141

PART V Foreign Affairs

EXERCISE 18 America's Role in the World..149

APPENDIX A Independent Projects
  Capital Punishment ♦ Gun Control 157
  Suicide ♦ Animal Rights ♦ Environmentalism 158
  Music and Politics 159

APPENDIX B Codebooks
  Short Label: ANES92 161
  Short Label: FIFTY 161
  Short Label: HOUSE 162
  Short Label: NORC93 162
  Short Label: OLDHOUSE 162
  Short Label: OLDSEN 163
  Short Label: P1973–93 163
  Short Label: SENATE 163
  Long Label: ANES92 164
  Long Label: FIFTY 166
  Long Label: HOUSE 170
  Long Label: NORC93 173
  Long Label: OLDHOUSE 178
  Long Label: OLDSEN 179
  Long Label: P1973-93 181
  Long Label: SENATE 182

License Agreement 184

PREFACE

The purpose of *AMERICAN GOVERNMENT: An Introduction Using MicroCase* is to introduce you to the real world of political science research: to give you a better understanding of American government by allowing you to explore our political system in ways impossible in standard textbooks. With this workbook and software—and with the assistance of a computer—you will explore the results of recent presidential elections as well as elections dating back to 1860. You will see who votes for whom, and why. Find out for yourself how much the news media influence elections. Take a close-up look at the men and women who serve in the House and Senate. What kinds of people are they? How do they vote? Where do they get their campaign funds, and how much do they spend? And what about issues? Where does the public stand on civil rights, civil liberties, taxes, confidence in government, abortion, and entitlements? Who refuses to vote for a woman or for an African American running for president? You will even be able to see how public opinion on many of these vital issues has changed (or stayed the same) from 1973 to 1993.

And it won't hurt a bit even if you have never used a computer before in your life! Everything you need to know about operating the computer or interpreting results you will learn effortlessly as you proceed through the workbook. Just follow along and soon you will be a good political science researcher, using the same tools used by professionals and the very best of the data sets available to them. There is nothing make-believe or "only educational" about this package. For example, your copy of the MicroCase Analysis System lets you use the finest analysis program ever developed for the micro computer, but you only have to deal with the features of the software appropriate for these assignments.

Finally, this book is meant to prepare you for future political science courses as well as for your participation in the American political system. As you go through the computer exercises, you will observe that there are many consistent patterns to the findings and that these reflect basic patterns of American politics. You will also discover that many of the commonly held beliefs about American government and politics simply aren't so, while some equally common beliefs do hold up.

What's New in the Third Edition
From the beginning we realized that this book had to be revised very often. There is a presidential election every four years and a new Congress every two years. But, the Congressional election of 1994 made us recognize that it was important that we bring out a new edition ahead of schedule to depict the first Republican-controlled House and Senate in 40 years. There simply was no way students would be happy analyzing data for the 103rd Congress, controlled by Democratic "powers" such as Tom Foley and Dan Rostenkowski who no longer even hold office.

In addition to creating entirely new House and Senate data files for the third edition and updating the congressional exercises, we retained data sets based on the previous House and Senate so that students could make some fundamental comparisons (see Exercise 13).

Disclaimer of Warranty: The licensor warrants that software is provided "as is" and without warranties as to performance or merchantability. Agents of the supplier may have made statements about this software. Any such statements do not constitute warranties and shall not be relied on by the licensee in deciding whether to use this program.

This program is provided without any express or implied warranties whatsoever. Because of the diversity of conditions and hardware under which this program may be used, no warranty of fitness for a particular purpose is offered. The licensee is advised to test the program thoroughly before relying on it. The licensee must assume the entire risk of using the program. Any liability of provider or manufacturer will be limited exclusively to product replacement.

The licensor shall not be liable for any expense, claim, liability, loss, or damage (including any incidental or consequential damage) either direct or indirect, by licensee from the use of the software.

Replacement Disk Policy: *MicroCase*® Corporation will replace any magnetic diskette that proves defective in materials or workmanship. To obtain a replacement copy, please ask your instructor or write to *MicroCase*® Corporation, 1301 120th Avenue N.E., Bellevue, WA 98005. You will be required to return the defective diskette in exchange for a replacement. Should you need to exchange the 5 1/4" diskettes for one that is 3 1/2" (or vice versa) send us your original diskette and $5. (Sorry, we cannot accept credit cards.)

ACKNOWLEDGMENTS

David Schultz served as the "consulting author" for the first two editions of this book. In that role he helped the MicroCase editorial staff select topics for exercises and find the most appropriate data bases. When it became clear that this book must be revised very frequently in order to remain current, especially vis-à-vis Congress, it also became clear that it would be more efficient for the staff to consult many political scientists on an ad hoc basis. We are grateful to Dr. Schultz for his previous help.

We also would like to acknowledge the contributions of many other people. First, we should acknowledge that it was Rodney Stark of the University of Washington who first developed the format for introducing students to real data analysis used by all of our introductory texts. We also must thank a number of institutions. The inclusion of selected variables from the 1992 American National Election Study would not have been possible without the generous permission of the Center for Political Studies, Institute of Social Research at the University of Michigan as well as the Inter-university Consortium for Political and Social Research. Thanks must also go to the National Opinion Research Center for its continued direction and administration of the U.S. General Social Survey, upon which many of these exercises are based. The Center for the American Woman and Politics at the Eagleton Institute of Politics at Rutgers University was also very helpful.

Finally, we would like to thank the following individuals who have contributed to this book in one way or another: Eric Uslaner, University of Maryland-College Park; Ron Rapoport, College of William and Mary; Matthew E. Wetstein, University of Evansville; Hal Barger and Tucker Gibson, Trinity University; William Flanigan, University of Minnesota; Nancy Kral, Tomball College; Chalmers Brumbaugh, Elon College; Robert Bradley, Illinois State University; Sara B. Crook, Peru State College; Jeri Cabot, College of Charleston; Roy Dawes, Gettysburg College; Martha Bailey, Old Dominion University; John B. Ashby, Northern Michigan University; John Berg, Suffolk University; Theresa Marchant-Shapiro, Union College; James Reed, College of St. Benedict; Robert Weber, St. John's University; Leonard Faulk, SUNY at Fredonia; Nancy Kindred, McNeil High School; Devin Bent, James Madison University; Lawrence W. Miller, Collin County College; Gary Aguiar, University of Hawaii at Hilo; Peter Maier, St. Norbert College; and Francie Mizell, Dekalb College.

INTRODUCTION

Welcome to the real world of political science research. There is nothing make-believe about what you will be doing with this student version of MicroCase. All of the data are real. In fact, these are some of the best data available to professional researchers and you will be using some of the same research techniques they use. By doing so, you will learn many things about American politics that previously only experts knew. Best of all, you can concentrate on results, not on learning how to use the software.

♦ EXERCISE 1 — GETTING STARTED ♦
Aspects of Federalism

In this exercise you will begin to discover the capacities of this student version of MicroCase and see how easy it is to operate. But first, a few general points can be helpful. This version of MicroCase requires an IBM-PC or fully compatible computer with a graphics card (preferably in color) and 640K of memory.

To begin, make sure your computer is at the DOS system prompt (which looks something like **C:>**). Then place the diskette in the A or B drive. If you placed the diskette in the A drive, *type* **A:** and *press* *<ENTER>*; if you placed the diskette in the B drive, *type* **B:** and *press* *<ENTER>*. Then *type* **MC** and *press* *<ENTER>*. (To use Student MicroCase on a computer with a monochrome display, you may need to start the program by *typing* **MC MONO** instead of MC.) It will take about 20 seconds to 30 seconds for the program to load.

Important: The first time you start Student MicroCase, you will be asked to enter your name. It is important to type your name correctly, since it will appear on all printed output. *Type your name* and *press* *<ENTER>*. If it is correct, simply *press* *<ENTER>* in response to the next prompt. (If you wish to correct a mistake, *type* **Y** at the prompt and *press* *<ENTER>*.) The copyright screen will appear. *Press* *<ENTER>* to continue.

MicroCase works from two primary menus. If you are using a color monitor, one menu is blue, the other is red. When you enter the program and pass beyond the title screen, by *pressing* *<ENTER>*, the blue menu will be on the screen. It looks like this:

```
%%%%%%%%%%%%%%%%  DATA AND FILE MANAGEMENT  %%%%%%%%%%%%%%%%

*S. Switch to STATISTICAL ANALYSIS MENU

  DATA MANAGEMENT:
    A. Define Variables/Recodes       E. Codebook
    B. Collapse Variables             F. Edit Variable Information
    C. Enter Data from Keyboard       G. Grading Recode
    D. List or Print Variable Values  H. Setup Data Entry

  FILE MANAGEMENT:
   *I. Open, Look, Erase or Copy File M. Move Data between Files
   *J. Create New Data File           N. Merge Files
    K. Create Subset File             O. Create Aggregation File
    L. Import/Export Data             P. Create Statistical Summary

*X. EXIT from MicroCase
```

Exercise 1: Aspects of Federalism

Notice that the highlight is on: **I. Open, Look, Erase, or Copy File**. This is the only task listed on this menu that is available in this version of the program, and that is why there is an asterisk to the left of the letter I. In order to analyze data, you must open a data file. So, *press* the *<ENTER>* key. The screen now displays the eight data files available to you: **NORC93, ANES92, FIFTY, HOUSE, OLDHOUSE, OLDSEN, SENATE**, and **P1973-93**. To open a file, place the highlight over its name and *press <ENTER>*. You can always move the highlight around by using the arrow keys.

When you have opened a data file and pressed <ENTER> to return to the blue menu, you will notice that the highlight is at the top of the screen on: **S. Switch To STATISTICAL ANALYSIS MENU**. To do this, just *press <ENTER>*. That is, you can always move from one menu to the other by placing the highlight on the **Switch To** line and *pressing <ENTER>*. Now you are on the red menu, which looks like this:

```
%%%%%%%%%%%%%   STATISTICAL ANALYSIS   %%%%%%%%%%%%%

*S. Switch to DATA AND FILE MANAGEMENT MENU

BASIC STATISTICAL ANALYSIS:
    A. Univariate Statistics        *F. Scatterplots
    B. Tabular Statistics            G. Correlation
    C. Analysis of Variance          H. Partial Correlation
    D. Covariance Analysis           I. Regression
   *E. Mapping Variables
ADVANCED STATISTICAL ANALYSIS:
    J. Regression Models             L. Factor Analysis
    K. Curve Fitting                 M. Logistic Regression
 Q. INTERACTIVE BATCH
*X. EXIT from MicroCase
```

Of these statistical functions, only four are available in this version of the software. You can recognize these by noting the asterisks to the left of the names. However, only two will be available at any given moment, depending on which data file you are using. In the exercises that follow, you will be introduced to each of these functions and learn how to use and interpret each.

When you are finished using MicroCase, simply put the highlight on **X. EXIT from MicroCase** and *press <ENTER>*. The exit command appears on both the red and blue menu.

Now, let's get started by examining some aspects of **federalism**—a system of government wherein two or more levels of government have formal authority over the same geographic area and the same citizens. Most Americans are governed by the national (or federal) government in Washington, DC, by a state government, and by county and city governments as well. Let's briefly trace how this system came into being.

In the beginning the "United" States were hardly united in any important sense of the word. Each state regarded its local government as sovereign, and relations among the states were defined as "a league of friendship and perpetual union" by the Articles of Confederation adopted by the Continental Congress in 1777 as a basis for pursuing the Revolutionary War. Under the Articles, each of the 13 states had one vote. There was no president or Supreme Court, and the decisions made by the Congress were not binding—states could observe them or not, as they saw fit.

Given the lack of any central power, the confederation worked very poorly. During the Revolution, General George Washington often lacked troops and supplies because individual states (called colonies then) often withdrew or refused to send their militias to fight and failed to provide money to sustain the war effort. Following the war, various economic and political crises led to growing support for a stronger central government. Eventually, this resulted in the Constitutional Congress, which gathered in Philadelphia in 1787 and designed a system of dual government. Under this system there would exist a national government with sufficient power to unite the nation, but its powers would be limited in a number of ways in order to preserve the independence of states, which would retain their own governments. The proponents of this system referred to it as federalism.

In the two centuries since the federal government was created, it has gained a great deal more power than was intended by those who drew up the Constitution and the power of the individual states has been curtailed. This has been particularly true in the area of taxation—in the beginning the federal budget was far smaller than the combined budgets of the states; today it is much larger. Moreover, the federal government does not treat all states the same in terms of where it spends its money or in its grants to state and local governments. Some states get back more from the federal government than they pay to it; others get back much less than they put in.

If you have not already done so, start the MicroCase program as described at the beginning of this exercise. With the highlight on **I. Open, Look, Erase, or Copy File** *press <ENTER>*. Using the arrow keys to move the highlight, place it on **FIFTY** and *press <ENTER>*. The screen will tell you that this data file is based on the 50 states and includes 75 variables. *Press <ENTER>* to return to the MENU. The highlight is now on the line reading **S. Switch To STATISTICAL ANALYSIS MENU**. *Press <ENTER>*. This menu is red. Place the highlight on **E. Mapping Variables** and *press <ENTER>*. Now the screen asks you for the name or number of the variable you wish to map. *Type* **2** and *press <ENTER>*.

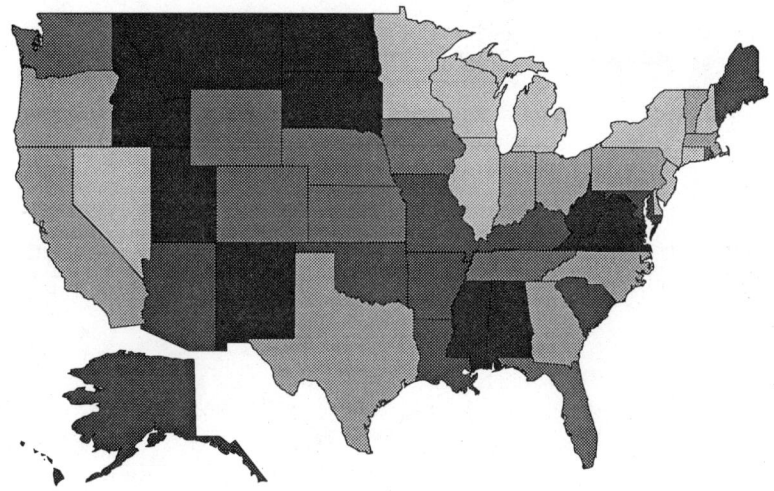

1989-1991: Net gain or loss of federal funds

A map of the United States appears on your screen, and the states appear in five colors from very dark to very light. The darker a state, the better deal it is getting from the federal government, getting back more than it pays in. The states shown in the lightest color have the worst exchange ratio with the federal government—they pay in more than they get back.

Now let's see which state is highest in terms of its exchange ratio with the federal government. *Type* **N** (for Name). The name New Mexico appears at the lower part of the screen and the state of New Mexico turns green.[1] Below the name we see that for every dollar that New Mexico sends to Washington it gets $2.02 back. *Press* the **down arrow** to move to the next highest state. Now the screen shows us that Mississippi was second highest, and if you keep pressing the down arrow you will be able to see the rate for each state as its name appears. However, if you want to see all 50 states ranked from high to low on their exchange ratio with the federal government, simply *type* **D** (for Distribution). Now you can see that 28 states get back more than they pay, while 2 states break even (1.00) and 20 states pay more than they get back. If you *press <ENTER>* or *type* **A** (for Area map) you will return to the map.[2]

Press <ENTER>. When the map disappears and the screen once again asks for the name or number of the variable to be mapped, type the name rather than the number of the variable. In this case *type* %**FED LAND** (be sure to leave a space between the D and the L) and *press <ENTER>*. (In fact you need only type enough of the variable name to make it unique and the computer will type the rest. So, in this case you could have simply typed %F and pressed <ENTER>.)

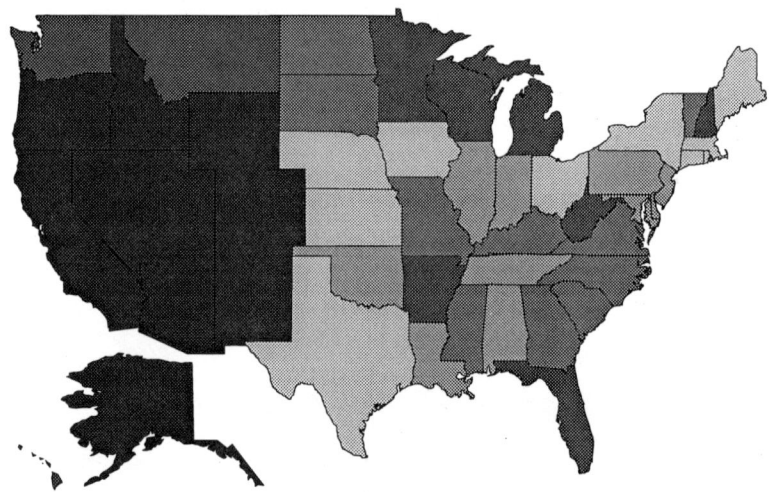

1990: Percent of state's area that is owned by the federal gov't.

This map shows the percentage of the land in each state that is owned by the federal government. The darkest states have the highest percentage of federal land ownership and all of them are in the West.

Again, let's see which state was highest. *Type* **N** (for Name). The name Nevada appears on the screen and an arrow points to the state of Nevada. Below the name we see that 82.74 percent of Nevada's land belongs to the federal government. That is, most of the state is controlled by Congress and federal agencies, not by the residents of Nevada. *Press* the **down arrow** to move to

---

[1] If your computer has CGA rather than VGA graphics, the state will not change color. Instead, a line will point to the state.

[2] If you have CGA graphics, you must *press <ENTER>* to return to the map.

the next highest state. Now the screen shows us that Alaska is second with two-thirds of its land under federal ownership, and if you keep pressing the down arrow you will be able to see the rate for each state as its name appears. Again, if you want to see all 50 states ranked from high to low simply *type* **D** (for Distribution). If you *type* **A** (for Area map) you will return to the map.

Simply by looking at the map you easily can see a very pronounced regional effect. That is, the states with the highest percentage of their land owned by the federal government are the relatively new states of the West. In the rest of the nation, the percentage of federal land is very low—less than 5 percent in most states. Many people in the western states resent having so much of their state owned by the federal government because this means that many important policies greatly affecting them are decided by members of Congress whose interests may be in conflict with the welfare of westerners or who may not understand local issues. This resentment in the West, which sometimes shows up clearly in elections, has been referred to as the "Sagebrush Revolt."

Press <ENTER>. When the map disappears and the screen once again asks for the name or number of the variable to be mapped, let's try a third technique. *Press* the **F3** key.

A window opens on the screen as shown below.

```
 1) CASE ID
 2) FED FUNDS
 3) %FED LAND
 4) FED.EMPLOY
 5) DEFENSE $
 6) CAP.PUNISH
 7) STATES '92
 8) %CLINTON '92
 9) %BUSH '92
10) %PEROT '92
11) STATES1988
12) %BUSH 1988
13) STATES '84
14) %REAGAN '84
15) STATES '72
16) %NIXON '72
17) STATES '64
```

This window shows you the name and number of every variable in any given MicroCase data file. The box to the right of it is a menu of commands you can use with this window. Use the **up** and **down arrow** keys to place the highlight on a given variable. The **page up** and **page down** keys will let you move more rapidly up and down the list. The **End** key will take you to the end of the list. The **Home** key will take you back to the beginning of the list. The **A** key will put the list of variable names in alphabetic order. The **G** key will let you type the number of any variable you wish and the highlight will shift to it. The **S** key will let you search the names and descriptions of all variables for a key word. If you type "federal," for example, the computer will indicate that word appears in three variables and it will show you which ones they are.

Exercise 1: Aspects of Federalism

Now place the highlight on the variable **4) FED.EMPLOY** and *press* the **right arrow** key. An additional window opens as shown below.

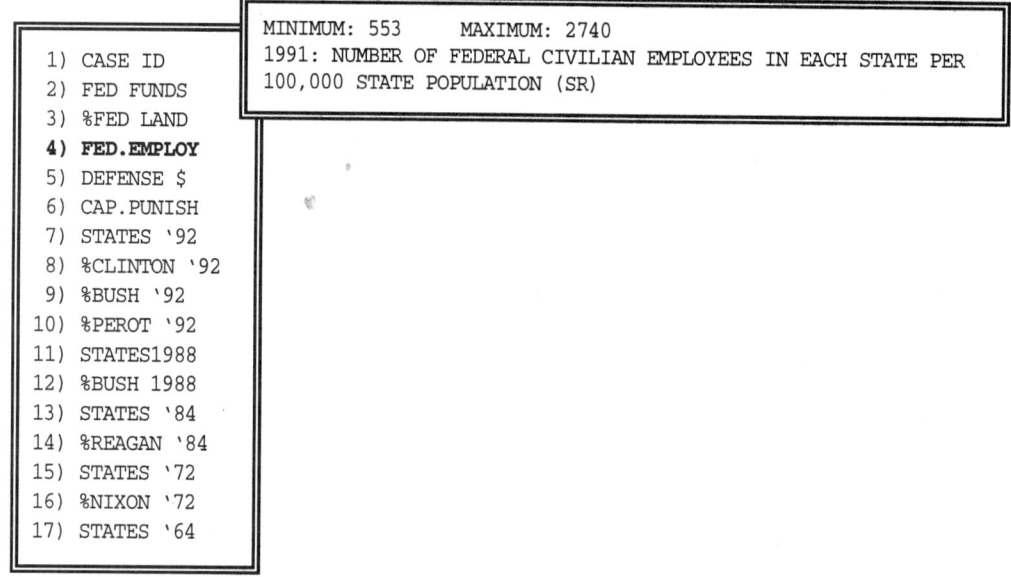

This window shows you the full description of the variable named **4) FED.EMPLOY**. This lets you know that this variable reports the number of federal civilian employees in each state per 100,000 state population. To close this window *press <ENTER>*. Now let's try a third way of selecting a variable to be mapped. With the highlight on **4) FED.EMPLOY** *press* the **left arrow** key. Notice that a checkmark appears next to the name of the variable. This indicates that you have selected it. Now *press <ENTER>*. A new map will appear on your screen.

Again a map of the states colors in. *Type* **D** (for Distribution). Now you can examine states from the highest to the lowest in terms of federal employees. Notice that the two highest states, Maryland and Virginia, both border on the District of Columbia. Many federal employees live in these two states and commute to D.C. But the next two highest states, Alaska and Hawaii, are the two states farthest from D.C. Both contain a number of federal installations.

In addition to the impact of the federal government on states, states and regions compete to exert control over the policies and procedures of the federal government. This is because states and regions differ greatly in terms of their resources, population profiles, and culture.

Type **A** to return to the map. The mapping function of MicroCase software has several features that are available only when you are using a computer with VGA graphics. To avoid confusion these functions appear across the bottom of the screen **only** if your computer has VGA graphics. The two functions are: **S:Spot** and **C:Comp** (for compare). If these two functions appear at the bottom of your screen, then you will want to go through the material below explaining how to use and interpret them.

With the map of **4** or **FED EMPLOY** still on the screen *press* the **S** key.

The map changes and a series of spots (or dots) of different sizes and colors appear, one dot for each state.

1991: Number of federal civilian employees in each state per 100,000 state population

The size of each spot is proportional to the value of each state on the variable being mapped. Thus Maryland and Virginia have the largest spots. The color keys remain as they were when the whole state was colored in. Many people find the spots easier to interpret than when only color cues are used.

By *pressing* **N** (for Name) you can discover the name and value of each case from highest to lowest; the spots turn green in succession just as whole states do.

With either a fully colored area map or a spot map on the screen, *press* **C** (for Compare). Now the map shrinks to half size and moves to the top of the screen. The screen asks: Name or number of variable for comparison. What this means is that you now can compare two maps by having both on the screen at the same time. *Type* **5** or **DEFENSE $** and *press <ENTER>*. The second map will appear and it will be either a spot map or a fully colored map, depending on the form of the map to which it is being compared.

Notice how very similar these two maps are. Government employment and government expenditures on defense tend to be high or low in the same places.

To clear the lower screen, *press <ENTER>* or *type* **C**. Again the screen asks for the name or number of the variable you wish to use for a comparison map. Use **35** or **LOBBYISTS** and *press <ENTER>*.

This map shows the number of registered lobbyists per state legislator, and it is quite unlike the map of federal employment.

To clear the screen *press <ENTER> twice* and you will be back to the full-size map. *Press <ENTER>* one more time and you can select a new map to use as the primary comparison map.

Whenever you wish to compare maps, you can do so most accurately by using the compare maps feature.

Exercise 1: Aspects of Federalism

In addition to the impact of federalism on states and regions, the states and regions exert considerable influence on the federal government. Moreover, because states and regions differ greatly in many ways—in resources, culture, and basic population profiles—there often is considerable conflict over federal policies. Now that you know how to use the mapping function, it is time for you to explore some key regional variations for yourself.

PART I

VOTERS AND ELECTIONS

In the exercises making up Part I we will examine presidential elections. What is the difference between electoral votes and popular votes? Who registers and votes? And who votes for whom? Along the way you will learn how to work the software and how to interpret your results.

♦ EXERCISE 2 ♦

Electoral and Popular Votes for President

Insert the diskette in either floppy drive of your computer. Change to the DOS prompt for that drive and *type* **MC** and *press* *<ENTER>* *twice*. With the highlight on **I. Open, Look, Erase, or Copy File** *press* *<ENTER>*. Using the arrow keys to move the highlight, place it on **FIFTY** and *press* *<ENTER>* *twice*. The blue menu reappears. The highlight is now on the line reading **S. Switch To STATISTICAL ANALYSIS MENU**. *Press* *<ENTER>*. This menu is red. Place the highlight on **E. Mapping Variables** and *press* *<ENTER>*. Now the screen asks you for the name or number of the variable you wish to map. *Type* **7** and *press* *<ENTER>*.

A map of the United States appears on your screen, and the states are colored red or yellow.

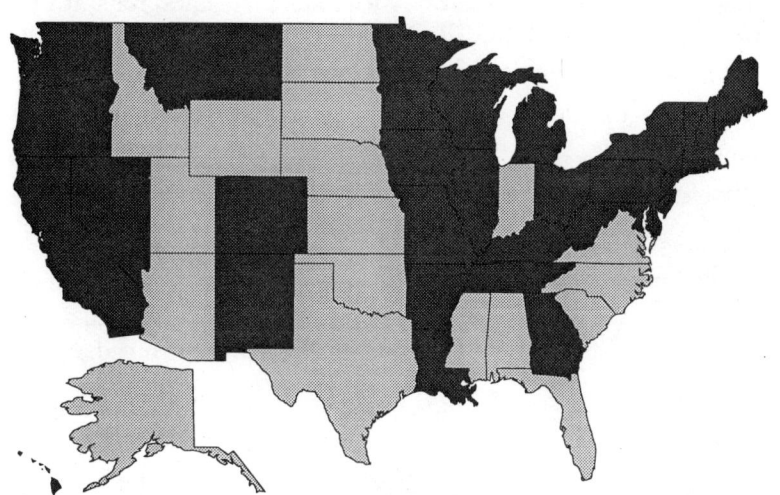

1992: Dark states won by Clinton, light states won by Bush

What you are seeing is the map of the electoral college vote for the 1992 presidential election. Bill Clinton, the Democrat, received the electoral votes of the dark red states, while George Bush, the Republican candidate, received the electoral votes of the states shown in yellow. The third candidate, Ross Perot, running as an independent, failed to win the electoral votes of any state. Clinton carried 32 of the 50 states and won by a large margin in the electoral college—370 to 168. This map of the electoral college vote makes it appear that Clinton was the overwhelming choice of the American people. However, since *all* of a state's electoral votes go to the candidate receiving the most votes cast by individual voters, comparisons based on electoral votes can make elections look much more lopsided than they might actually have been in terms of popular vote. In principle, Clinton might have won each of the 32 states by one vote, while losing by huge margins in each of the other 18. In fact, when there are more than two candidates involved, a state's electoral votes may all be won by someone who received far less than a majority of the votes cast.

Press <ENTER>. When the map disappears and the screen once again asks for the name or number of the variable to be mapped, type **8** or **%CLINTON92** and *press <ENTER>*.

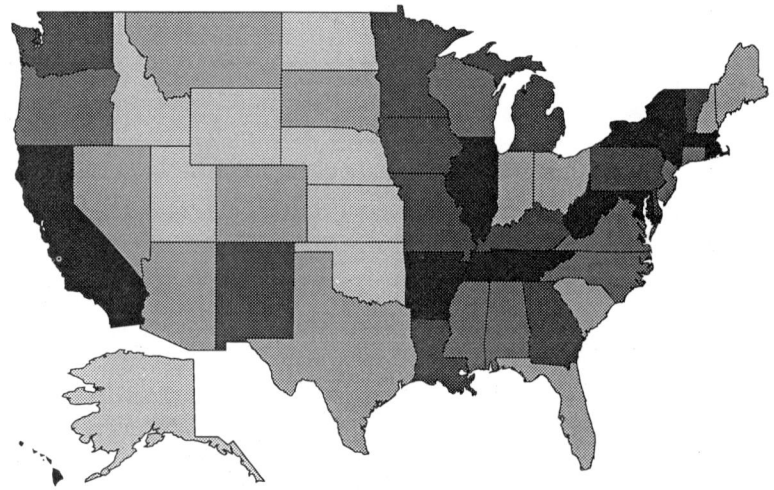

1992: Percent of votes for Clinton (Dem.)

This map shows the percentage of the vote won by Clinton. The darker a state, the higher its percentage of Clinton voters. The states in dark red are those that gave Clinton his strongest support. The lighter states gave Clinton the weakest support.

Now let's see which state was highest. *Type* **N** (for Name). The name Arkansas appears on the screen and the state of Arkansas turns green. Below the name we see that 54 percent of Arkansas' voters supported their governor for president. *Type* **D** (for Distribution).

Here we see that besides Arkansas, Clinton received half or more of the votes in only two other states: New York and Maryland. In all other states he received fewer than half of the votes cast—often far fewer. In fact, Clinton received only 43 percent of the total national votes for president. *Press <ENTER>* until you are prompted for another variable to be mapped.

Now map **10** or **%PEROT 92**. This map helps us understand how Clinton could win the election although most American voters did not support him. In many states, large numbers of voters voted for neither major party candidate and supported Ross Perot instead. The map shows that these voters were highly concentrated in the western states (and perhaps Perot tapped western resentment to federal policies as discussed in Exercise 1).

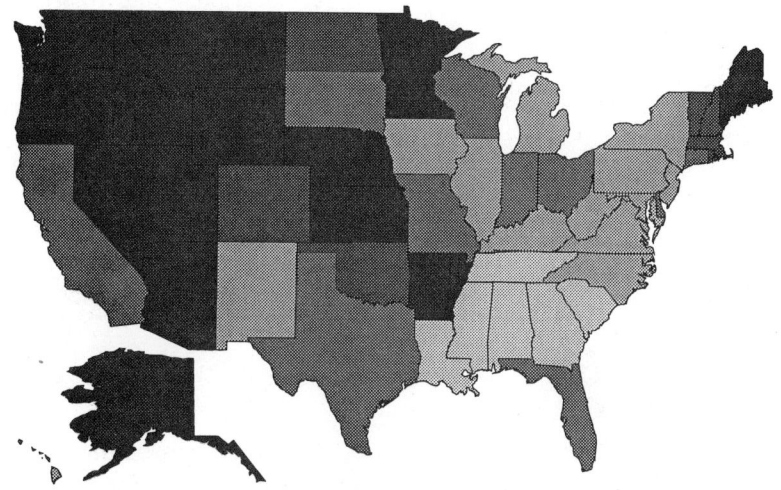

1992: Percent of votes for Perot (Indep.)

Type **D** (for Distribution). Here we see that Perot received 30 percent of the votes in Maine, closely followed by Utah (29%) and Idaho (28%). Amazingly, Perot received 24 percent of the votes in Arkansas.

You may wonder why presidents aren't simply elected by direct popular vote—why the candidate who receives the greatest number of votes nationwide isn't declared the winner? This takes us back to federalism. When the Constitution was written small states were fearful that large states would simply ignore their particular needs and concerns and push through laws most favorable to their own self-interests. That is why the House of Representatives is apportioned on the basis of population, so some states have many representatives, while other states have only one, but each state has two senators. The electoral college was also meant to somewhat limit the power of the most populous states. Each state received the number of electoral votes equal to its total number of senators and representatives. Thus no state can have fewer than 3 electoral votes. As a result, small states have somewhat more impact on electoral votes than they do on the total popular vote.

Now let's look at another presidential election. Map **11** or **STATES 1988**.

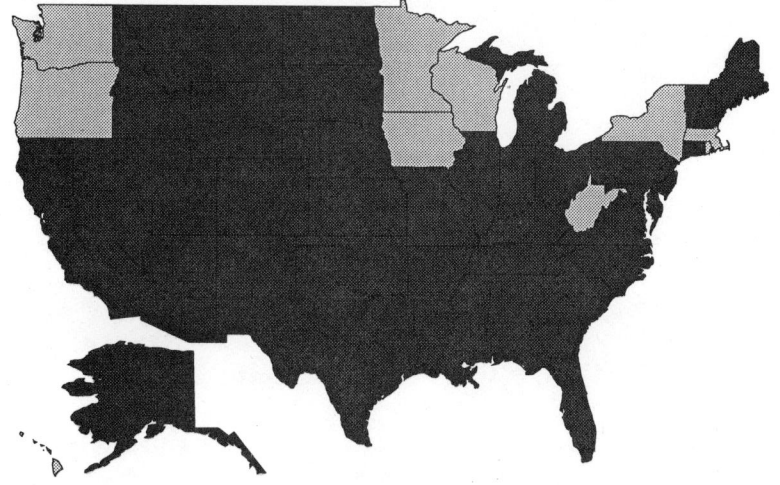

1988: Dark states carried by Bush (Rep.), light ones by Dukakis (Dem.)

Exercise 2: Electoral and Popular Votes for President

This map shows the electoral college vote in the 1988 election, when George Bush carried 40 states with 426 electoral votes while his Democratic opponent Michael Dukakis, the governor of Massachusetts, carried only 10 states with 112 electoral votes. Despite the fact that Bush's victory over Dukakis in the electoral college was by a far greater margin than Clinton's victory over Bush four years later, Michael Dukakis got 45 percent of the vote cast in 1988, Bill Clinton received only 43 percent in 1992. And that makes it even clearer how much Perot's candidacy influenced the outcome.

To see this more clearly, simply *press <ENTER>* and when the screen asks for the name or number of the variable to be mapped, use any of the three methods described in the first exercise to select **12** or **%BUSH 1988**.

The darkest states are, of course, those in which Bush had the largest margin; notice that they are mainly in the Mountain States—the same states where Perot ran so strongly four years later. Utah gave Bush his biggest margin (67.4%). But even in Rhode Island where Bush ran his weakest race, he got a larger percentage of the vote (43.9%) than Clinton's national total in 1992.

Ross Perot was not the first, or even the most successful, "third party" candidate for president. As you will see, there have been many such candidates including Abraham Lincoln, who was elected when the Republicans were a third party. During the 1920s various leftist parties ran presidential candidates. Select **23** or **% LEFT '20**.

In 1920 the combined vote for the Socialist and the Farmer-Labor Party candidates was highest in Washington (21.7%). In South Carolina, Louisiana, and Idaho they received less than 0.1 percent and therefore are listed as having gotten 0 percent of the vote. Notice, however, that three states are colored blue and are listed as –99: Hawaii, Alaska, and Vermont. –99 is the missing data code. There were no votes cast for president in Hawaii and Alaska in 1920 because they weren't states. And there were no votes cast for either leftist candidate in Vermont that year because they had been unable to get on the ballot. Whenever a state shows up as blue and has the value –99 on any variable, that means no data are available for that state on that variable.

Your turn.

◆ EXERCISE 3 ◆
Voter Participation

Once again open the **FIFTY** data file and go to the mapping function. This time create the map for variable **31** or **%REGIST.92**. This is a map of the proportion of the persons of voting age who are registered to vote. All told, 68.2 percent of Americans of voting age were registered in 1992. *Press* **N** (for Name) to see which state was highest.

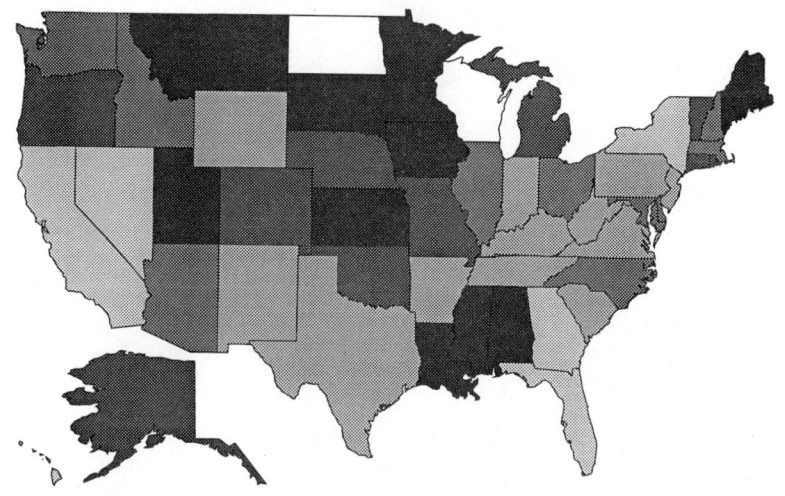

1992: Percent registered to vote (N. Dak. & Wisc. don't have registration)

Minnesota is highest with 86.1 percent of its voting age population registered. *Press* the **down arrow** to see the next highest state. Maine is second with 85.4 percent registered. Now *press* **D** (for Distribution) to see all 50 states ranked from high to low. Notice that Wisconsin and North Dakota have the value of –99. That means they have no registration rates (since –99 always means missing data). The reason these two states lack rates is because they do not require voters to register. Notice how low the rate is in California where only 57.6 percent are registered.

Not only have many Americans failed to register to vote, many of those who are registered fail to vote in any particular election. To see this, create a map for variable **28** or **% VOTED '92**.

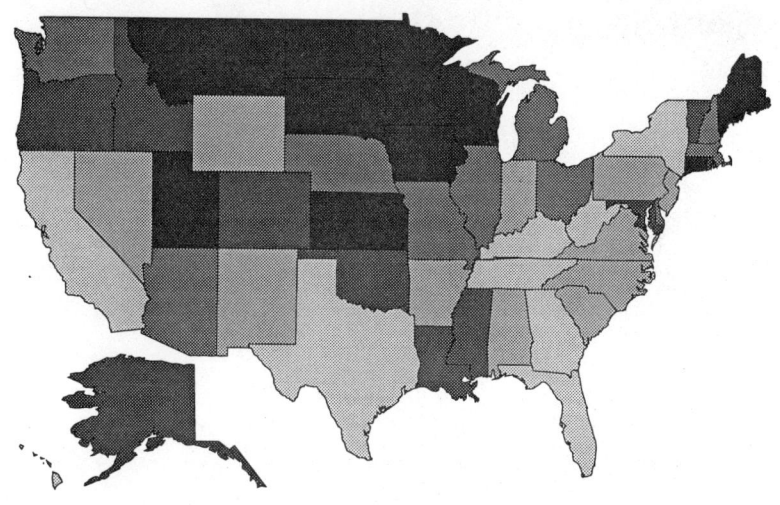

1992: Percent of total population who voted

Exercise 3: Voter Participation

Overall, 61.3 percent of Americans cast ballots in the presidential election that year—when Bill Clinton defeated George Bush. *Press* **D** (for Distribution). Wisconsin had the highest voter turnout in 1992 (75.3), followed by Minnesota (74.2%). California (52.8%) had the lowest turnout, followed by Georgia (54.1%). If you have VGA graphics, you may wish to use the compare map function here.

Now create the same map for the 1980 election: **30** or **%VOTED '80**.

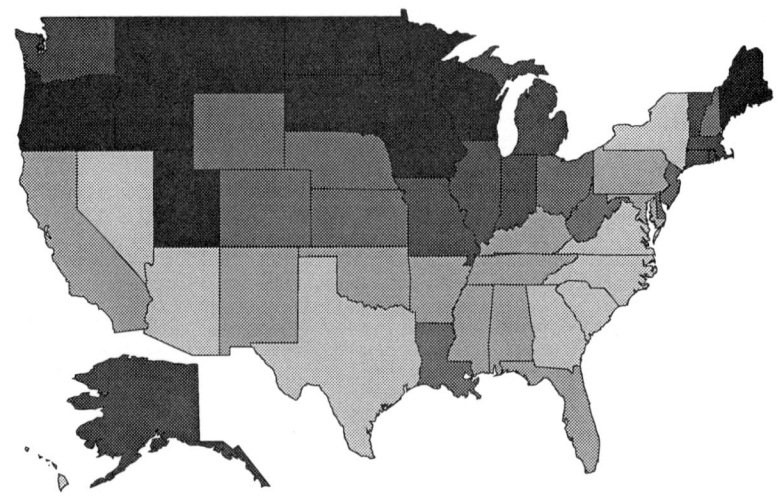

1980: Percent of voting age population who voted in the presidential election

Notice how very much alike these two maps are. This shows that patterns of voter turnout are quite stable over time, the same states being high or low from one election to the next.

It is easy to notice when two maps are this much alike. But as maps become somewhat less alike it often is difficult to say how much alike they are. For example, is the map for **66** or **KINKO'S** a lot like the maps for voter turnout, or just somewhat like them, or not too much like them?

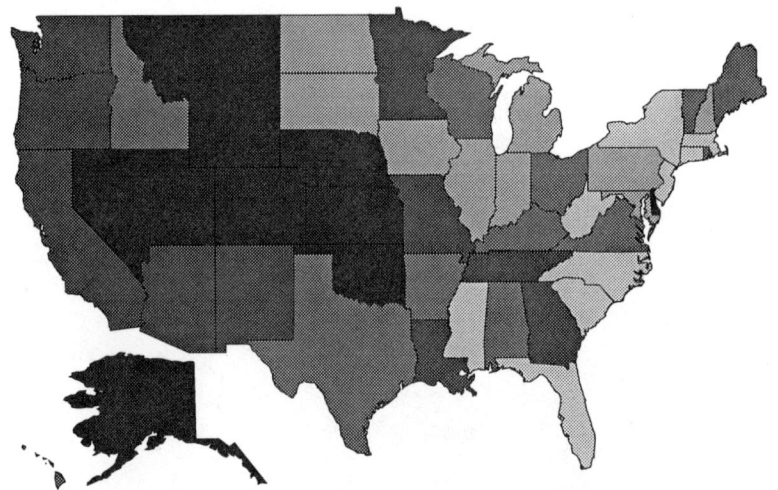

1989: Kinko's copy centers per 100,000 population

It also becomes more difficult to say how alike any two maps are when the maps are very complex. For example, it would be much harder to compare two maps based on the 3,142 counties of the United States than two maps based on the 50 states. The same is true of attempts to compare lists. It was not too hard to compare the distributions of the 1980 and 1988 voter turnouts and to notice that the same states tended to be high or low both times. But it would have been much harder with a longer list. Thus it was a considerable achievement when, in the 1890s, an Englishman by the name of Karl Pearson discovered an incredibly simple method for comparing maps or lists.

To see Pearson's method, let's use the maps of voter registration and voter turnout for 1992 as the maps we wish to compare. The first thing we do is draw a horizontal line across the bottom of a piece of paper. We will let this line represent the map of voter registration in 1992. So, at the left end of this line we will write 57.6, which indicates the state with the lowest registration: California. At the right end of the line we will place the number 86.1 to represent Minnesota as the state with the highest registration.

$$\overline{}$$
57.6   86.1

Now we can draw a vertical line up the left side of the paper. This line will represent the map of voter turnout in 1992. At the bottom of this line we will write 52.8 to represent California, the lowest state that year. At the top we will write 75.3 to represent Wisconsin.

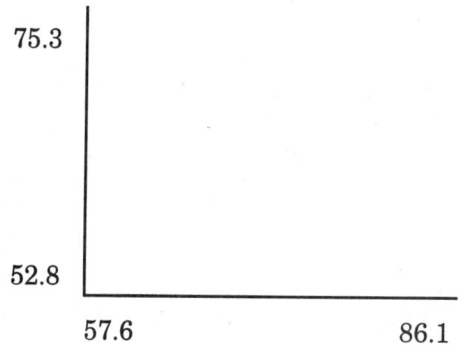

Now that we have a line with an appropriate scale to represent each map, the next thing we need to do is refer to the distributions for each map in order to learn the value of each state and then locate it on each line according to its score. Let's start with Minnesota. First let's locate Minnesota on the horizontal line representing registration in 1992. Since it was the highest state we can easily find it on the line, and we can draw a vertical line up from its position on 1992 registration. Next we can locate Minnesota on the vertical line representing the map of the percent who voted in 1992. Minnesota was second highest with a percentage of 74.2. So we can estimate its position as slightly below that of the top state, Wisconsin, and then draw a horizontal line out from its position. Where these two lines meet (or cross) we can make a dot. This dot represents the combined map location of Minnesota.

Next, let's locate South Dakota. Its voter registration was 80.1 percent in 1992, so we can make a mark on the horizontal line at that spot. In 1992 South Dakota's voter turnout was 70.2 percent, so we can mark that point on the vertical line. Now we draw a line up from the mark on the horizontal line and draw one out from the mark on the vertical line. Where these two lines intersect is the combined map location for South Dakota.

When we have followed this procedure for each state, we will have a dot for each state located within the space defined by the vertical and horizontal lines representing the two maps. What we have done is to create a **scatterplot**. Fortunately, you don't have to go to all this trouble. *MicroCase* will do it for you. Return to the red **STATISTICAL ANALYSIS** screen and select the

F. Scatterplot function. Make **28** or **%VOTED '92** the dependent variable and *press <ENTER>*. Now make **31** or **%REGIST.92** the independent variable and *press <ENTER> twice*. This screen will appear:

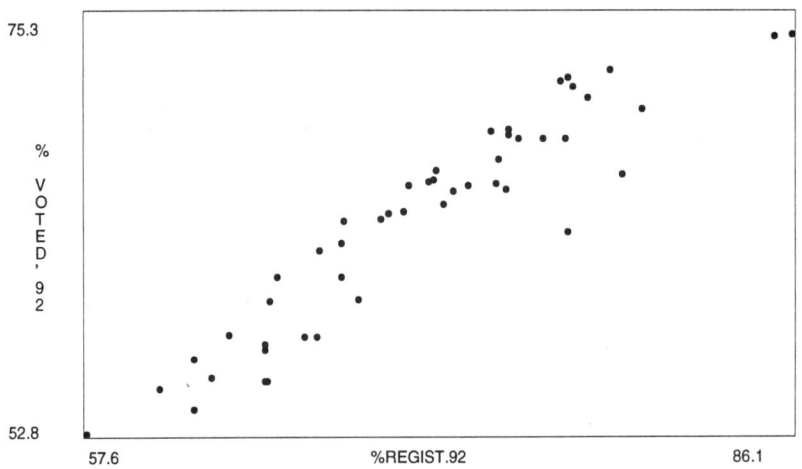

Current: r = 0.936   Prob. = 0.000   N = 48   N Miss. = 2

reg. **L**ine   **R**esid   **O**utliers   **S**how case   **X** label   **Y** label   **P**rint

Each of these dots is a state. *Press* **S** (for Show case) and then *type* **UTAH** and *press <ENTER>*. See the dot that is flashing on the screen? That dot represents Utah's combined position on the two maps. *Press <ENTER>* to cause the dot to stop flashing. You can examine the dot for each state in this way. To leave the Show case function simply *press <ENTER> again*. If you have forgotten precisely what either of the two maps represents, you can examine their long labels by *pressing* **X** for the horizontal map and **Y** for the vertical map. (To close the windows containing long labels, *press <ENTER>*.)

Once Pearson had created a scatterplot, his next step was to calculate what he called the **regression line**. To see this line simply *press* **L** (for Line). This line represents the best effort to draw a straight line that connects all of the dots. It is unnecessary for you to know how to calculate the location of the regression line—the program does it for you. But, if you would like to see how the regression line would look if all of the dots were along a straight line, all you need to do is examine the scatterplot for identical maps. So, if you create a scatterplot using **28** or **% VOTED '92** as both the dependent and independent variables, you will be comparing identical maps and the dots representing states will all be on the regression line like a string of beads.

However, since the maps for **28** or **% VOTED '92** and for **31** or **%REGIST.92** are only very similar, but not identical, some of the dots are scattered near, but not upon, the regression line. Pearson's method for calculating how much alike are any two maps or lists is very easy, once the regression line has been drawn. What it amounts to is measuring the distance out from the regression line to every dot. To do this, simply *press* **R** (for Residual). See all the little lines. If you added them all together you would have a sum of the deviation of the dots from the regression line. The smaller this sum, the more alike are the two maps. For example, when the maps are identical and all the dots are on the regression line, the sum of the deviations is 0.

In order to make it simple to interpret results, Pearson invented a procedure to convert the sums into a number he called the **correlation coefficient**. The correlation coefficient varies from 0.0

to 1.0. When maps are identical the correlation coefficient will be 1.0. When they are completely unalike, the correlation coefficient will be 0.0. Thus, the closer the correlation coefficient is to 1.0 the more alike the two maps or lists. Pearson used the letter **r** as the symbol for his correlation coefficient. Look at the lower left corner of the screen and you will see **r = 0.936**. This is almost perfect—you will seldom find coefficients this large.

The point of calculating correlations is to discover links between various social phenomena. Suppose we suspected that hunting is a symptom of a culture of violence and that where there is a lot of hunting the murder rate will also be high. This claim cannot be true unless there is a substantial correlation between **75** or **MURDER** and **72** or **HUNTING**. So create this scatterplot. (First *press <ENTER>* to return to the prompt requesting your variable choices.)

This scatterplot reveals that correlation coefficients can be either positive or negative. We have been examining positive correlations—where voter registration rates are higher, voter turnouts are higher too. That is, as one rises so does the other—they tend to occur in unison. But, here we discover that our hunch about a link between hunting and murder is not supported by the evidence—in fact, the reverse would seem to be true. Notice that in this scatterplot the regression line (*press* **L**) slopes downward from left to right, rather than upward. That always indicates a negative correlation. And notice that a minus sign now precedes the correlation coefficient –0.453. This occurs because where a larger percentage of a state's population hunts, the murder rate tends to be lower. They vary together, but in opposite directions.

Keep in mind that correlation and causation are not the same thing. It is true that without correlation there can be no causation. Thus voter registration could not be considered as a possible cause of voting if there were no correlation between the two. But, correlations often occur between two variables without one being a cause of the other. For example, in any grade school you would find a very high correlation between children's height and their reading ability. This correlation occurs because both height and reading ability reflect age—the taller kids are older and the older kids read better. The negative correlation between hunting and homicide might also be a noncausal correlation. Hunting is most common in rural states with large wilderness areas, and the style of life in such communities tends to result in low rates of violence, including murder.

Finally, let's see a scatterplot of two variables that are not correlated. Use **44** or **SUICIDE** as the dependent variable and **68** or **% BEER** as the independent variable. Are suicide rates higher in states where beer is the alcoholic beverage of preference? No. The relationship between these two variables is essentially random. The dots are scattered all over the screen. *Press* **L** (for Line). The regression line has no slope and simply crosses the screen from left to right. And the correlation coefficient is a minuscule .015.

Now, it's your turn to create and interpret some scatterplots.

WORKSHEET

NAME:

COURSE:

DATE:

EXERCISE 3

Workbook exercises and software are copyrighted. Copying is prohibited by law.

1. Open the **FIFTY** data file and select the **scatterplot** function. Create the following scatterplot:

    Dependent variable: **34** or **BLACK LEGL**
    Independent variable: **50** or **% BLACK**

    Write down the long label for **BLACK LEGL**:
    (Press **Y** to see it and *press <ENTER>* to close the window)

    _____

    What is the correlation coefficient? r = _____

    Is this a positive or negative correlation? (circle one) POS   NEG

    Suggest a reason why this correlation exists.

2. Create the following scatterplot:

    Dependent variable: **9** or **%BUSH '92**
    Independent variable: **12** or **%BUSH 1988**

    What is the correlation coefficient? r = _____

    Is this a positive or negative correlation? (circle one) POS   NEG

3. Create the following scatterplot:

    Dependent variable: **12** or **%BUSH 1988**
    Independent variable: **14** or **%REAGAN 84**

    What is the correlation coefficient? r = _____

    Is this a positive or negative correlation? (circle one) POS   NEG

Exercise 3: Voter Participation

WORKSHEET	EXERCISE 3

4. Create the following scatterplot:

   Dependent variable: **10** or **%PEROT 92**
   Independent variable: **37** or **N.REV./NAT**

   Write down the long label for **N.REV./NAT**: (Press **X** to see it)

   _____

   What is the correlation coefficient? r = _____

   Is this a positive or negative correlation? (circle one) POS   NEG

   Suggest a reason why this correlation exists.

5. Create the following scatterplot:

   Dependent variable: **8** or **%CLINTON92**
   Independent variable: **41** or **% BAPTIST**

   Write down the long label for **% BAPTIST**: (Press **X** to see it)

   _____

   What is the correlation coefficient? r = _____

   Is this a positive or negative correlation? (circle one) POS   NEG

   Discuss this correlation in light of the fact that Clinton is a Baptist.

| NAME | EXERCISE 3 |

6. Create the following scatterplot:

   Dependent variable: **47** or **PLAYBOY**
   Independent variable: **42** or **CH.MEMBERS**

   Write down the long label for **PLAYBOY**: (Press **Y** to see it)

   _____

   Write down the long label for **CH.MEMBERS**: (Press **X** to see it)

   _____

   What is the correlation coefficient?   r = _____

   Is this a positive or negative correlation? (circle one)   POS   NEG

   Suggest a reason why this correlation exists.

7. Create the following scatterplot:

   Dependent variable: **46** or **FLD&STREAM**
   Independent variable: **45** or **PICKUPS**

   Write down the long label for **FLD&STREAM**: (Press **Y** to see it)

   _____

   Write down the long label for **45** *or* **PICKUPS**: (Press **X** to see it)

   _____

   What is the correlation coefficient?   r = _____

   Is this a positive or negative correlation? (circle one)   POS   NEG

   Suggest a reason why this correlation exists.

Exercise 3: Voter Participation

WORKSHEET	EXERCISE 3

8. Create the following scatterplot:

    Dependent variable: **47** or **PLAYBOY**
    Independent variable: **62** or **%MALE HOME**

    Write down the long label for **%MALE HOME**: (Press **X** to see it)

    _____

    What is the correlation coefficient?   r = _____

    Is this a positive or negative correlation? (circle one)   POS   NEG

    Suggest a reason why this correlation exists.

9. Create the following scatterplot:

    Dependent variable: **68** or **% BEER**
    Independent variable: **48** or **GOURMET**

    Write down the long label for **% BEER**:
    (Press **Y** to see it and *press <ENTER>* to close the window)

    _____

    Write down the long label for **GOURMET**: (Press **X** to see it)

    _____

    What is the correlation coefficient?   r = _____

    Is this a positive or negative correlation? (circle one)   POS   NEG

    Suggest a reason why this correlation exists.

♦ EXERCISE 4 ♦
Exploring Election Polls: Who Votes?

Long before anyone even is nominated for president, the press is full of public opinion polls that report who the public favors at that moment. These pre-election polls are based on the science of sampling, but they also involve some artful guesses and even some luck. In this exercise we are going to explore two major election surveys to see why surveys work and to understand their limitations. Let's begin with the science and then see how art and luck enter in.

Political scientists usually call public opinion polls *survey research*. The basis for all such research is **random sampling**. That is, if we want to know what percentage of Americans favor a particular candidate, like rap music, or support freedom of speech we are not required to ask *everyone*. If we were, there would be no polls because not even the government could afford to interview more than 200 million people. But, in fact, so long as we select persons randomly to be interviewed—that is, use means of selection which give everyone an equal chance of being selected—then results based on such a random sample can be generalized to the whole population. That is, the laws of probability allow us to calculate the odds that the sample accurately reflects the population that was sampled. Several things influence the accuracy of samples. The most important is size. Political scientists prefer samples of at least 1,000 individuals, and samples including 1,500 to 2,000 or more persons are even more accurate. Nevertheless, all samples are subject to some random or chance variations. These random variations are always of concern to pollsters, and later in this exercise we will see how researchers take them into account. However, election surveys involve even more serious limits.

The trouble is, surveys tell us how the *whole population* feels about various political candidates, but the whole population never votes—as we saw in the last exercise. Often, the political views of those who do vote are significantly different from the views of those who fail to vote so that in order to accurately predict an election the researchers must eliminate the non-voters. That's where art and luck enter in. We simply don't know for sure ahead of time who will and who will not vote. From years of experience pollsters have gotten pretty good at figuring out the odds that particular sorts of people will vote—but this varies depending on how close the race is, how much people care who wins, and even on less predictable things such as the weather. For example, it is well-known that bad weather on election day favors Republican candidates because Republican voters are more likely than Democrats to vote and this difference increases when bad weather discourages less regular voters. So, all attempts to use polls to reveal voting patterns are subject to these non-random fluctuations.

Today we are going to examine two nationwide surveys of the 1992 election conducted by two of the most respected survey organizations in the United States. By comparing their results we can gain firsthand experience with some of the problems involved in election polling.

Start MicroCase and go to the blue menu for **DATA AND FILE MANAGEMENT**. Place the highlight on **I. Open, Look, Erase, or Copy File** and *press <ENTER>*. Now place the highlight on **NORC93** and *press <ENTER>* to open this file.

The screen tells you that you have opened data selected from the 1993 General Social Survey (GSS), which consists of a national sample of 1,606 Americans aged 18 and over, each of whom was interviewed at length. The GSS is conducted nearly every March by the National Opinion Research Center (NORC) at the University of Chicago—the GSS is funded by the National Science Foundation. NORC conducts many other national surveys each year. *Press <ENTER>* to return to the menu.

Go to the **STATISTICAL ANALYSIS MENU** (the red menu) and place the highlight on the **Univariate Statistics** function and *press <ENTER>*. Use **3** or **VOTE 92?** as the variable. When the screen asks for a subset variable, simply *press <ENTER>* to continue. This screen will appear:

In 1992, you remember that Clinton ran for President on the Democratic ticket against Bush for the Republicans and Perot as an Independent. Do you remember for sure whether or not you voted in that election?

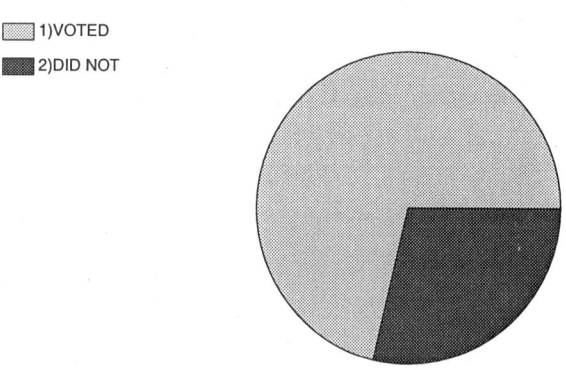

1) VOTED
2) DID NOT

Press **D** (for Distribution)[1]. This distribution will appear:

	FREQUENCY	%
VOTED	1109	71.3
DID NOT	446	28.7

Here we see that 1,109 persons, or 71.3 percent of the sample, said they had voted while 446, or 28.7 percent, said they had not. Recall from the previous exercise that according to data prepared by the U.S. Bureau of the Census, only 61.3 percent of Americans of voting age actually voted in the 1992 election. Why the big difference? There are several reasons why the survey suggests a higher level of voting. First, the data in Exercise 2 did not subtract those ineligible to vote, while the survey did. Secondly, some people who did not vote will report having done so when asked by an interviewer, especially those who usually do vote, but who missed that election for one reason or another. Some people are unwilling to admit to an interviewer that they didn't live up to the standards defining good citizenship. Finally, persons least likely to vote also are least likely to be found by survey interviewers or to agree to be interviewed—migrant workers, the homeless, the mentally ill, persons in jail or engaged in illegal activities, and the like. Thus surveys are always a bit biased in favor of the more affluent and settled population.

Press <ENTER> twice to clear the screen and then use **1** or **PRES IN 92** as the variable. When the screen asks for a subset variable, simply *press <ENTER>* to continue. This screen will appear:

---

[1] If you have CGA graphics, *Press* **T** (for Table).

IF VOTED: Did you vote for Clinton, Bush or Perot?

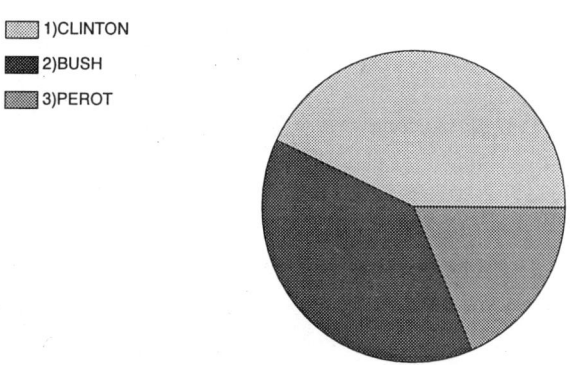

Press **D** (for Distribution). This distribution will appear:

	FREQUENCY	%
CLINTON	464	43.0
BUSH	416	38.5
PEROT	200	18.5

Here we see that 43 percent reported they voted for Clinton. This is exactly the percentage for Clinton in the actual national vote—the survey is precisely correct. Moreover, the Bush and Perot vote reported in this survey is within 0.5 percent of the actual results—Bush got 38 percent and Perot 19 percent. Thus, despite being inaccurate in reporting the percentage who voted, the survey got the votes right even though it was asking people about how they had voted five months earlier.

Now, open the **ANES92** data set. The screen informs you that this is a national sample of 2,487 Americans (18 and over) interviewed by the Institute for Social Research of the University of Michigan in 1992, as part of the American National Election Study. In fact, the interviewing began one week following the election. Like NORC, the Michigan Institute for Social Research is a famous survey research institute and it has been pre-eminent in voting studies over the past 40 years.

Using the **Univariate Statistics** function let's examine **1** or **VOTE? 92** as the variable.

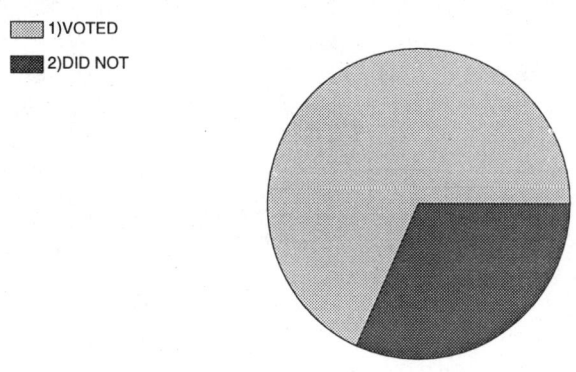

Exercise 4: Exploring Election Polls: Who Votes?

Press **D** (for Distribution). This distribution will appear:

	FREQUENCY	%
VOTED	1689	68.2
DID NOT	787	31.8

Here we see that 68.2 percent claimed to have voted. This also is too high (only 61.3 percent actually voted), but it is closer to the actual percentage than is the NORC estimate we just examined. Perhaps that is because the Michigan data were gathered immediately after the election.

Now let's examine who people said they voted for. Use **2** or **PRES IN 92** as the variable. This screen will appear:

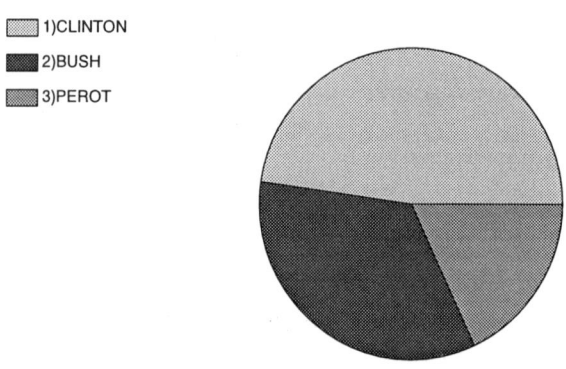

Press **D** (for Distribution). This distribution will appear:

	FREQUENCY	%
CLINTON	793	47.8
BUSH	564	34.0
PEROT	301	18.2

The Michigan survey found that Clinton received 47.8 percent of the vote, with 34 percent going to Bush and 18.2 percent for Perot. The Perot estimate is very accurate (he actually received 19%), but the Clinton estimate is too high (Clinton got only 43%) and the Bush estimate is too low (he actually got 38%). Why the discrepancy? The experts at the Michigan Institute for Social Research who conducted the study think that in the immediate aftermath of the Clinton victory, some people probably decided to claim they had backed the winner, when they had not done so. This caused a slight overestimate of Clinton's vote. But then, after Clinton took office his popularity fell quite rapidly, so that by the time the NORC interviews were conducted, people were more willing to admit they had not voted for Clinton; hence the NORC results were more accurate.

But there is a second, very important reason for the disagreements between poll results. Samples only *estimate* the distribution of some trait such as voting behavior in a population, and these estimates are subject to random fluctuation. That is, when people are selected randomly to be interviewed, purely by chance a few more Clinton voters, or red-heads, or smokers, or whatever can be selected. You may have noticed that stories in the news media based on survey results often mention that the results are only accurate within a particular percentage range. For example, the NORC results are expected to be within 2 percentage points (plus or minus) of the actual distribution, or what we would find if we asked everyone. This range is referred to as the **confidence interval**. Thus, when we see that a survey found that 43 percent of those interviewed said they voted for Clinton, this could be off by as much as 2 percentage points in either direction on the basis of random variation alone. That is, the true percentage could be as high as 45 or as low as 41.

A substantial part of the Michigan overestimate of the Clinton vote probably is due to random fluctuations. When this happens in a poll taken before the election and used to predict the winner, it is very embarrassing for the polling organization. However, when the data are to be used to better understand who voted and why they voted as they did, small random fluctuations such as this turn out not to be very important.

So, now let's see what we can find out about who voted and who didn't and whether both surveys give the same results on these questions.

Return to the **STATISTICAL ANALYSIS MENU** and place the highlight on **Tabular Analysis** and *press <ENTER>*. When the screen asks for the name or number of the row variable *type* **1** and *press <ENTER>*. When it asks for the name or number of the column variable *type* **30**. Or, instead you could *type* **VOTE? 92** for the row variable and then *type* **SEX** for the column variable. When the screen asks for a control variable, simply *press <ENTER>*. When it asks for a subset variable, simply *press <ENTER>*.

This table is now on your screen:

	MALE	FEMALE
VOTED	794	895
DID NOT	359	428
TOTAL	1153	1323

Across the top are the labels: MALE and FEMALE. Down the side are the answers each respondent who was eligible to vote gave to the question whether or not they had voted in the 1992 election: VOTED and DID NOT. The numbers within the table reflect the numbers of persons of each sex who said they voted or did not vote. (Six men and 5 women failed or refused to answer the question and are classified as missing. Cases having missing data are always ignored in the calculations and therefore are not included in the total number of cases shown at the bottom of each column.)

Looking at the table we see that of the 1,153 males who were eligible to vote in 1992, 794 said they voted and 359 said they did not vote. Looking at the next column of the table we see that there were a lot more voters among women—895. But there were far more non-voters among women too. That's because the sample accurately represents the nation's population, and thus there are far more female than male respondents—older Americans being very disproportionately female.

This makes it obvious that we can't simply compare raw numbers of voters. We must take differences in the size of populations into account. To do so, we can calculate the **percentage** of voters and non-voters in each sex. To do that, simply *press* **C** for column percentages. The column percentages are added to the table:

Exercise 4: Exploring Election Polls: Who Votes?

	MALE	FEMALE
VOTED	68.9	67.6
DID NOT	31.1	32.4
TOTAL	100.0	100.0

Here we see that men were slightly more likely to say they voted. To see this, read the table from left to right just as you read ordinary text, and compare percentages. Thus, 68.9 percent of males said they had voted, while 67.7 percent of females had done so. Or, comparing across the lower row of the table we can see that 31.1 percent of males did not vote compared with 32.4 percent of females. Of course, these differences are very small. Small differences raise questions for survey data analysis.

As already mentioned, **random sampling** is the basis of all survey research because the laws of probability allow us to **calculate the odds** that something observed in the sample accurately reflects a feature of the population sampled—subject to **two limitations**.

First of all, the sample must be sufficiently **large**. Obviously, we couldn't use a sample of two people as the basis for describing the American population—there is a very high probability that they both would be white. For this reason, survey studies include enough cases so that they can accurately reflect the population in terms of variations in such characteristics as age, sex, education, religion, and the like. The accuracy of a sample is a function of its size: the larger the sample, the more accurate it is. Good survey studies are based on 1,000 cases or more—the American National Election Study is based on 2,487 Americans.

The second limitation has to do with the **magnitude of the difference** observed in a table. Because samples are based on the principle of random selection, they are subject to some degree of random fluctuation. That is, for purely random reasons there can be small differences between the sample and the population as was the case with the percent who voted for Clinton. Thus, whenever we examine cross-tabulations such as those shown above, social scientists always must ask whether what they are seeing is a real difference—one that would turn up if the entire population were examined—or only a random fluctuation, which does not reflect a true difference in the population.

The small size of the gender difference observed above (on a sample this size) will always make an experienced analyst suspicious that it is merely the result of random fluctuations.

Fortunately, there is a very simple technique for calculating the odds that a given difference is real or random. This calculation is called a **test of statistical significance**. Differences observed in samples are said to be statistically significant when the odds against random results are high enough. There is no mathematical way to determine just how high is high enough. But through the years social scientists have settled on the rule of thumb that they will ignore all differences unless the odds are at least **20 to 1** against their being random. Put another way, social scientists reject all findings when the probability they are random is greater than .05, or 5 in 100. What this level of significance means is that if 100 random samples were drawn independently from the same population, a difference this large would not turn up more than 5 times, purely by chance. In fact, many social scientists think this is too lenient a standard and some even require that the probability that a finding is random be less than .01, or 1 in 100. To apply these rules of thumb, social scientists calculate the **level of significance** of the differences in question and compare them against these standards.

Let's see what the level of significance is for this table. *Press* **S** (for Statistics). Across the screen, under the words **Nominal Statistics**, we see: Chi-Square: 0.419 DF: 1 (Prob. = 0.517).

Chi square is the name of the particular test of significance we are using. You can ignore everything else except (Prob. = 0.517), which translates as: the probability that this is a random, not real, result is only 0.517. Put another way, this means that if there is no gender difference in voting in the population as a whole, we would expect an observed difference this large by sheer chance 517 times out of every 1,000 random samples, or more than half of the time. So the odds are very high that males and females did not differ in their tendency to vote in 1992. In any event, the level of significance falls very short of the minimal .05 level. That is, we shall reject any finding when the probability is *larger* than 0.05.

Press <ENTER> twice and you will be ready to run a new table. This time let's use the F3 window to select the variables. *Press* the **F3** key. Place the highlight on variable **1** and *press* the **left arrow** to select it as the **row variable**. Now use the **down arrow** to place the highlight on **11** or **READ PAPER** and *press* the **left arrow** key to select it as the **column variable**. Now *press <ENTER>*. The two indicated variables will take their place on the screen as the row and column variables. *Press <ENTER> twice* and the table will appear. *Press* **C** for column percentages.

	DAILY	WEEKLY	SELDOM
VOTED	76.5	70.3	52.8
DID NOT	23.5	29.7	47.2

Here we see (by reading across and comparing) that people who read a newspaper every day were far more likely (76.5) than those who read the paper only weekly (70.3) or seldom (52.8) to have voted.

Again, to see the level of significance *press* **S**. Here the probability is far smaller than our standard of 0.05—it is 0.000. That means the odds of getting a finding this large through random errors are less than 1 chance in 1,000 samples.

Press <ENTER> twice and you will be ready to run a new table. Again use **1** or **VOTE? 92** as the row variable and use **22** or **FAMILY $** as the column variable. *Press* **C** for column percentages.

	UNDER $12K	$12–$25K	$25–$40K	$40–$60K	OVER $60K
VOTED	49.4	65.0	73.7	78.1	82.3
DID NOT	50.6	35.0	26.3	21.9	17.7

See the flashing arrow at the upper right? It is to warn you that the table extends beyond the edge of the screen. You may use the left and right arrow keys to move portions of the table onto and off the screen. This lets you see that the higher their family income, the more likely people were to have voted. Thus only about half of those with annual incomes of $12,000 or less said they voted, while about 82 percent of those with incomes over $60,000 voted.

Again, to see the level of significance *press* **S**. Here the probability is far smaller than our standard of 0.05—it is 0.000. That means the odds of getting a finding this large through random errors are less than 1 chance in 1,000 samples.

Although social scientists rely primarily on the Chi-square test of significance to decide which findings are sufficiently large to be taken seriously, they also make some use of the correlation coefficient, which we examined in Exercise 3. However, for survey data they tend to prefer a coefficient known as Cramer's V. Directly under the line reading **Chi-Square** is **V: 0.246**. Cramer's V also varies from 0.0 (for no correlation) to 1.0 (for a perfect correlation). Correlations based on survey data tend to be lower than those based on aggregate units such as the 50 states. Thus, this correlation would be considered quite high by social science researchers. In any event, Chi-square will tell you when V is large enough to be significant.

Now let's create another cross-tabulation. This time use **1** or **VOTE? 92** as the row variable and for the column variable use **31** or **REGION**. Remember to *press* **C** for column percentages. Recall from Exercise 3 that voter turnouts are lower in the South. The same seems to be true in this table.

	EAST	MIDWEST	SOUTH	WEST
VOTED	68.9	75.4	59.7	73.1
DID NOT	31.1	24.6	40.3	26.9

But is this difference large enough to be significant? *Press* **S** and see. Yes. The probability shown on the screen (Prob. = 0.000) is far smaller than our standard of 0.05.

Significance applies to all correlations, not just to those based on survey data. If you turn back to Exercise 3 and examine the scatterplot between voting in 1992 and in 1980, you will see Prob. = 0.000. That means there is less than 1 chance in 1,000 that this correlation occurred by chance. Questions about whether tests of significance are appropriate when no sample is involved (as it is not here—**all** 50 states are included, not a random subset), await you in a statistics class. In these exercises you should treat a scatterplot as showing no relationship between the variables when the probability of random error is greater than 0.050.

Press <ENTER> twice to run a new table. Again use **1** or **VOTE? 92** as the row variable and use **21** or **UNIONIZED?** as the column variable. *Press* **C** for column percentages.

	UNIONIZED	NON-UNION
VOTED	77.2	66.5
DID NOT	22.8	33.5

Here we see that union members were more likely than non-members to vote in 1992. But is this difference large enough to be significant? *Press* **S** and see. Yes. The probability shown on the screen (Prob. = 0.000) is far smaller than our standard of 0.05.

Let's see if this finding is the same in the **NORC93** data set. Go to the blue menu for **DATA AND FILE MANAGEMENT**. Place the highlight on **I. Open, Look, Erase, or Copy File** and *press <ENTER>*. Now place the highlight on **NORC93** and *press <ENTER>* twice to open this file. Return to the **Tabular Statistics** option and use **3** or **VOTE 92?** as the row variable and **20** or **UNIONIZED?** as the column variable. *Press* **C** for column percentages.

	UNIONIZED	NOT UNION
VOTED	80.6	69.7
DID NOT	19.4	30.3

In the NORC sample the same fundamental finding appears: union members are more likely to have voted. *Press* **S** and you will see that the probability is very small that this could be a random finding. Thus, even though the percentages aren't exactly the same in the two surveys, the findings are consistent between the two.

Now, it's your turn to explore these data sets.

WORKSHEET

NAME:

COURSE:

DATE:

Workbook exercises and software are copyrighted. Copying is prohibited by law.

EXERCISE 4

1. With the **NORC93** data file open, select the **Tabular Statistics** option. Now make **3** or **VOTE 92?** the row variable and **18** or **FAMILY $** the column variable. *Press* **C** for column percentages. Fill in the table below based on the table shown on your screen. **(Remember to use the arrow keys to see the entire table.)**

	UNDER $12K	$12–$23K	$23–$35K	$35–$60K	OVER $60K
VOTED	%	%	%	%	%
DID NOT	%	%	%	%	%

Which income group was most likely to have voted? _____

Which income group was least likely to have voted? _____

Is the difference statistically significant? (circle one)   YES   NO

Prob. = _____

What is the value of Cramer's V?   V = _____

Is this finding consistent with the **ANES92** data? (circle one)   YES   NO

2. Now make **3** or **VOTE 92?** the row variable and **7** or **AGE** the column variable. *Press* **C** for column percentages. Fill in the table below.

	18–29	30–39	40–49	50–65	OVER 65
VOTED	%	%	%	%	%
DID NOT	%	%	%	%	%

Which age group was most likely to have voted? _____

Which age group was least likely to have voted? _____

Is the difference statistically significant? (circle one)   YES   NO

Prob. = _____

What is the value of Cramer's V?   V = _____

Exercise 4: Exploring Election Polls: Who Votes?

| WORKSHEET | EXERCISE 4 |

3. This time let's see if education matters. Make **3** or **VOTE 92?** the row variable and **17** or **EDUCATION** the column variable. *Press* **C** for column percentages. **(After this I will no longer tell you to use column percentages, you ought to know by now.)** Fill in the table below.

	LESS HIGH SCHOOL	HIGH SCHOOL GRAD	SOME COLLEGE	COLLEGE GRAD
VOTED	%	%	%	%
DID NOT	%	%	%	%

Which education group was most likely to have voted? _____

Which education group was least likely to have voted? _____

Is the difference statistically significant? (circle one)   YES   NO

Prob. = _____

What is the value of Cramer's V?   V = _____

4. Now let's compare people who support different political parties. The row variable is **3** or **VOTE 92?** and the column variable is **85** or **DEM/REP**. Fill in the table below.

	DEMOCRAT	REPUBLICAN
VOTED	%	%
DID NOT	%	%

Which group was most likely to have voted? _____

Which group was least likely to have voted? _____

Is the difference statistically significant? (circle one)   YES   NO

Prob. = _____

What is the value of Cramer's V?   V = _____

NAME	EXERCISE 4

5. Were frequent church attenders more likely to vote? The row variable: **3** or **VOTE 92?**; column variable: **13** or **CH. ATTEND**.

	WEEKLY	MONTHLY	YEARLY	SELDOM/NEV
VOTED	%	%	%	%
DID NOT	%	%	%	%

Which group was most likely to have voted? _____

Which group was least likely to have voted? _____

Is the difference statistically significant? (circle one)   YES   NO

Prob. = _____

What is the value of Cramer's V?   V = _____

6. Were veterans of the armed forces more likely to vote? The row variable: **3** or **VOTE 92?**; column variable: **15** or **VETERAN?**.

	VETERAN	NON-VET
VOTED	%	%
DID NOT	%	%

Which group was most likely to have voted? _____

Which group was least likely to have voted? _____

Is the difference statistically significant? (circle one)   YES   NO

Prob. = _____

What is the value of Cramer's V?   V = _____

7. Were people who like heavy metal music more likely to vote? The row variable: **3** or **VOTE 92?**; column variable: **38** or **HVY METL**.

	LIKES	MIXED	DISLIKES
VOTED	%	%	%
DID NOT	%	%	%

Exercise 4: Exploring Election Polls: Who Votes?

WORKSHEET	EXERCISE 4

Which group was least likely to have voted? _____

Is the difference statistically significant? (circle one)   YES   NO

Prob. = _____

What is the value of Cramer's V?   V = _____

8. Now, look back over the seven tables you have created and select the one that *you* find the most interesting—perhaps because a difference you expected to turn up did not, or one you didn't expect, did. Then, discuss this finding in detail, speculating on what this particular table suggests about American voters.

◆ EXERCISE 5 ◆
Who Votes for Whom?

We have seen that people who vote differ in many ways from those who don't. Now let's see if people differ depending on who they vote for.

Open the **ANES92** data set and go to the cross-tabulation (**Tabular Statistics**) function. Use **2** or **PRES IN 92** as the row variable and **24** or **CATH/PROT** as the column variable. *Press <ENTER> twice* to skip the control variable and subset option. *Press* **C** for column percentages. This table will appear:

	CATHOLIC	LIB.PROT	CONS.PROT.
CLINTON	49.6	40.8	48.9
BUSH	30.3	38.8	39.2
PEROT	20.1	20.5	11.9

It appears that Clinton ran most strongly among Catholics and members of conservative Protestant denominations, and did worst among liberal Protestants. Are these differences significant? *Press* **S** (for Statistics). Yes. Since Prob. = 0.000, there is less than 1 chance in 1,000 of getting differences this large by chance. Cramer's V is 0.092. At first glance, this finding would puzzle most political experts. Despite the fact that Clinton claims membership in the Southern Baptist Convention, one of the nation's more conservative Protestant bodies, it is widely believed that it is conservative Protestants, not liberal Protestants, who most favored President Bush. After thinking about this table a moment or two, experienced voting analysts would realize what was behind these results. To understand for yourself, use **2** or **PRES IN 92** as the row variable and **29** or **WH/AFRIC.A** as the column variable. (Don't forget to percentage your table.)

	WHITE	AFRICAN-AM
CLINTON	41.2	92.9
BUSH	37.7	4.9
PEROT	21.1	2.2

This table shows that African Americans voted almost unanimously for Bill Clinton. For a variety of historical reasons, African Americans also are almost unanimously members of conservative Protestant denominations.

When both of these findings are considered, they explain the apparently lower level of support for Bush among conservative Protestants. The inclusion in this group of a substantial number of black voters who strongly supported Clinton made it appear that the conservative Protestants in general were less likely to support Bush.

Now, let's untangle race and religion. Use **2** or **PRES IN 92** as the row variable and **24** or **CATH/PROT** as the column variable. When the screen asks for a control variable, *type* **29** or **WH/AFRIC.A** and *press <ENTER> three times. Press* **C** for column percentages. This table will appear:

WH/AFRIC.A: WHITE

	CATHOLIC	LIB.PROT	CONS.PROT.
CLINTON	45.6	37.5	30.9
BUSH	31.6	40.2	52.7
PEROT	22.8	22.3	16.4

Notice on the top line that this table is limited to white respondents and that among them conservative Protestants are the group most, rather than least, likely to have voted for Bush. The difference is highly significant (Prob. = 0.000).

Press <ENTER> to view the table including only African-American voters. *Press* **C** for column percentages.

WH/AFRIC.A: AFRICAN-AM

	CATHOLIC	LIB.PROT	CONS.PROT.
CLINTON	91.7	89.7	94.5
BUSH	8.3	10.3	2.8
PEROT	0.0	0.0	2.8

Before trying to interpret this table, look at the total number of cases on which each column of percentages is based. There are only 12 African-American Catholic voters in the sample. Similarly, there are only 29 black liberal Protestants in the sample. We cannot base estimates of the voting behavior of black Catholics on a sample of 12. Nor can we assess black liberal Protestants on the basis of 29 cases.

Press **S** (for Statistics). Notice that Prob. = 0.355. As explained in Exercise 4, significance is based not only on the *size* of the correlation, but also on *the number of cases* on which the correlation is based.

Here we have discovered a problem that often hampers survey research. If African Americans are included in a sample in proportion to their percentage of the population, a sample must be quite large in order for there to be a sufficient number of African Americans to permit satisfactory analysis. In this case we have learned that, by examining only white voters, the expected tendency for Bush to receive his greatest support from conservative Protestants appears. But we are unable to examine religious differences among African-American voters because of the tiny numbers of Catholics and liberal Protestants.

Now use **2** or **PRES IN 92** as the row variable and **30** or **SEX** as the column variable and this table will appear—once you *press* **C** for column percentages.

	MALE	FEMALE
CLINTON	42.5	52.5
BUSH	34.8	33.3
PEROT	22.6	14.2

Here we see that had only men voted, Bush and Perot would have run stronger races. Clinton ran very strongly among women.

Suppose for some reason we wished to examine this relationship among white voters only. We have seen above how to use race as a control variable to create two tables, one for whites and one for African Americans. But since we aren't interested in seeing two tables, we can use a different technique. Use **2** or **PRES IN 92** as the row variable and **30** or **SEX** as the column variable. But this time just *press <ENTER>* when the screen asks for a control variable. Now, when the screen asks for a subset, *type* **29** or **WH/AFRIC.A** and *press <ENTER>*. Now the screen asks for the lower limit. *Type* **1** (the category for whites) and *press <ENTER>*. When the screen asks for the upper limit, *type* **1** again and *press <ENTER>*. When the screen asks for a second subset variable, simply *press <ENTER>*. Again, *press* **C** for column percentages.

SUBSET WITH VALUE WHITE

	MALE	FEMALE
CLINTON	36.3	45.7
BUSH	38.4	37.1
PEROT	25.3	17.2

The table that appears is like the one shown for all respondents, above, except the phrase **SUBSET WITH VALUE WHITE** is across the top. This indicates that the table is limited to a subset of the sample, namely, white respondents. The subset feature can be used to limit any table to certain values on some variable. For example, we could subset on sex and examine only men (make 1 the lowest and highest values) or only women (make 2 the lowest and highest values).

Now, let's see more about who voted for whom. During the campaign, there was some discussion of the methods used by Bill Clinton to avoid being drafted during the Vietnam War. Respondents in the Michigan election study were asked: *Do you think that most men who tried to avoid military service during the Vietnam War should have served regardless of their personal beliefs?* The public was about evenly split on this issue: 48.3 percent said yes and 51.7 percent said no. Let's see if this issue hurt Clinton.

Now use **2** or **PRES IN 92** as the row variable and **20** or **DRAFT** as the column variable and this table will appear—*press* **C** for column percentages.

	YES	NO
CLINTON	35.6	59.0
BUSH	47.0	21.6
PEROT	17.5	19.5

The issue did damage Clinton. Among those who thought it wrong to avoid the draft during the Vietnam War, George Bush won by a large margin—47 to 35.6. Among those who thought it okay to avoid the draft, Clinton won easily—59 to 21.6.

Finally, use **2** or **PRES IN 92** as the row variable and **3** or **WHO IN 88** as the column variable and this table will appear—*press* **C** for column percentages.

	BUSH	DUKAKIS
CLINTON	23.6	83.1
BUSH	55.0	5.2
PEROT	21.4	11.8

Exercise 5: Who Votes for Whom?

Here we see the key to Bush's defeat. Of those who voted for him in 1988, nearly half (45%) deserted him in 1992—going about equally to Perot and to Clinton. Of those who voted for the Democrat Dukakis in 1988, the vast majority voted for Clinton and far fewer defected to Perot than was true of Bush voters.

Your turn.

WORKSHEET

NAME:

COURSE:

DATE:

EXERCISE 5

Workbook exercises and software are copyrighted. Copying is prohibited by law.

1. Switch to the **NORC93** data set and, using the **Tabular Statistics** option, create and fill in the table below. Row variable: **1** or **PRES IN 92**; column variable: **20** or **UNIONIZED?**. (Remember to percentage all of your tables in this exercise.)

	UNIONIZED	NOT UNION
CLINTON	%	%
BUSH	%	%
PEROT	%	%

Who won among union members? _____

Prob. = _____

What is the value of Cramer's V?   V = _____

2. Create and fill in the table below. Row variable: **1** or **PRES IN 92**; column variable: **26** or **GUN OWNER?**.

	HAS GUN	NO GUN
CLINTON	%	%
BUSH	%	%
PEROT	%	%

What is the long label for variable 26? (Open the F3 window to see it.) _____

_____

Who won among gun owners? _____

Prob. = _____

What is the value of Cramer's V?   V = _____

Exercise 5: Who Votes for Whom?

| WORKSHEET | EXERCISE 5 |

3. Create and fill in the table below. Row variable: **1** or **PRES IN 92**; column variable: **18** or **FAMILY $**.

	UNDER $12K	$12–$23K	$23–$35K	$35–$60K	OVER $60K
CLINTON	%	%	%	%	%
BUSH	%	%	%	%	%
PEROT	%	%	%	%	%

In which group did Clinton gain the greatest support? _____

In which group did Clinton gain the least support? _____

In which group did Bush gain the greatest support? _____

In which group did Bush gain the least support? _____

Prob. = _____

What is the value of Cramer's V?   V = _____

4. Create and fill in the table below. Row variable: **1** or **PRES IN 92**; column variable: **21** or **HAPPY?**.

	VERY HAPPY	PRET.HAPPY	NOT TOO
CLINTON	%	%	%
BUSH	%	%	%
PEROT	%	%	%

What is the long label for variable 21? (Open the **F3** window to see it.) _____

_____

_____

Which candidate did the happiest voters support? _____

Which candidate did the least happy voters support? _____

Prob. = _____

What is the value of Cramer's V?   V = _____

NAME

EXERCISE 5

Could there be a connection between the results about income and these about happiness? Explain.

5. Create and fill in the table below. Row variable: **1** or **PRES IN 92**; column variable: **33** or **COUNTRY&W**.

	LIKES	MIXED	DISLIKES
CLINTON	%	%	%
BUSH	%	%	%
PEROT	%	%	%

What is the long label for variable 33? _____

_____

In which group did Clinton gain the greatest support? _____

In which group did Bush gain the greatest support? _____

Prob. = _____

6. Create and fill in the table below. Row variable: **1** or **PRES IN 92**; column variable: **75** or **VEGGIE?**.

	OFTEN	SOMETIMES	NEVER
CLINTON	%	%	%
BUSH	%	%	%
PEROT	%	%	%

What is the long label for variable 75? _____

_____

In which group did Clinton gain the greatest support? _____

Exercise 5: Who Votes for Whom?

WORKSHEET	EXERCISE 5

In which group did Bush gain the greatest support? _____

Prob. = _____

On the basis of the two tables on this page, contrast Clinton and Bush supporters.

7. Make **1** or **PRES IN 92** the row variable, and *any* variable of *your choice* as the column variable and see how it influenced voting. Explain why you chose this variable and report your results by drawing the table, filling it in, and reporting whether it is significant.

Part I: Voters and Elections

◆ EXERCISE 6 ◆
Elections and the Media

For most Americans, election campaigns are media events, and this is especially true of presidential elections. Although the candidates travel constantly, very few voters actually see them in person. In fact, a major point of all the campaign travel is to get extensive coverage by the local news media where they appear.

In principle, media coverage of election campaigns can have three primary results. First, the media can create *interest*. Second, they can *inform* voters about issues and candidates. Third, they can *influence* voter perceptions and choices. Let's examine each of these possibilities.

Open the **ANES92** data set and go to the **Univariate Statistics** function and *press <ENTER>*. Use **9** or **TV NEWS?** as the variable. When the screen asks for a subset variable, simply *press <ENTER>* to continue. After the pie chart appears, *press **D*** (for Distribution). This distribution will appear:

How many days in the past week did you watch the news on TV?

	FREQUENCY	%
EVERY DAY	1105	47.9
4–6 DAYS	392	17.0
2–3 DAYS	427	18.5
1 OR NONE	383	16.6

About half of Americans claimed to have watched TV news every day. *Press <ENTER> twice* to select a new variable.

Next, use **10** or **TV PREZ** as the variable. When you *press **D*** (for Distribution), this distribution will appear:

How much attention did you pay to news on TV about the campaign for President?

	FREQUENCY	%
VERY MUCH	445	21.9
MUCH	658	32.4
SOME	638	31.4
NOT MUCH	293	14.4

Only a fifth of Americans expressed "very much" interest in TV news about the presidential campaign, and altogether about half were particularly interested.

Use **11** or **READ PAPER** as the variable. When you *press **D*** (for Distribution), this distribution will appear:

Exercise 6: Elections and the Media

About how often do you read a daily newspaper?

	FREQUENCY	%
DAILY	910	39.4
WEEKLY	832	36.0
SELDOM	566	24.5

Clearly, more Americans depend upon TV than upon newspapers for their news. Only 4 in 10 read the paper every day.

Use **12** or **TALK SHOWS** as the variable. When you *press* **D** (for Distribution), this distribution will appear:

Do you listen to or watch shows on radio or TV where people call in to voice their opinions?

	FREQUENCY	%
YES	1264	54.8
NO	1044	45.2

The majority of Americans listen to or watch talk shows.

Now, let's find out about being interested and informed.

Use **4** or **INTEREST?** as the variable. When you *press* **D** (for Distribution), this distribution will appear:

Interviewer's rating of the respondent's level of interest in the campaign.

	FREQUENCY	%
MUCH	962	38.8
SOMEWHAT	1085	43.8
NOT MUCH	430	17.4

Since interviewers spent several hours with each respondent and covered a large number of political questions, they were in a good position to provide an overall assessment of interest. They rated about 4 of 10 as having much interest in the campaign.

Interviewers also were asked to rate each respondent's general level of information about politics (whether or not they needed to have many questions explained to them, for example).

Use **8** or **INFORMED?** as the variable. When you *press* **D** (for Distribution), this distribution will appear:

	FREQUENCY	%
HIGH	1123	45.2
AVERAGE	872	35.1
LOW	489	19.7

The interviewers thought about half of Americans were well informed and scored them as high. They scored only about 20 percent as poorly informed.

Now let's find out if the media influence whether people are interested in campaigns.

Switch to the **Tabular Statistics** function and create this table: Use **4** or **INTEREST?** as the row variable and **9** or **TV NEWS?** as the column variable. *Press <ENTER> twice and the following table will appear—press* **C** *for column percentages.*

	EVERY DAY	4–6 DAYS	2–3 DAYS	1 OR NONE
MUCH	49.8	41.8	27.5	18.8
SOMEWHAT	36.4	47.7	54.5	45.8
NOT MUCH	13.8	10.5	18.1	35.3

People who watch TV news daily are far more likely (49.8%) to have been scored as much interested in the campaign than are those who seldom or never watch TV news, only 18.9 percent of whom were scored as much interested. This is no surprise. However, it doesn't necessarily show that media exposure *causes* people to become interested in a political campaign. It is equally plausible that the more interested people are (for whatever reason) the more likely they are to watch the news on TV. In reality, probably both things take place—the more interested watch more often and watching builds up interest. *Press <ENTER> to clear this table.*

Now use **4** or **INTEREST?** as the row variable and **10** or **TV PREZ** as the column variable and this table will appear—*press* **C** *for column percentages.*

	VERY MUCH	MUCH	SOME	NOT MUCH
MUCH	78.7	51.5	20.0	13.4
SOMEWHAT	16.5	44.3	63.7	37.7
NOT MUCH	4.8	4.3	16.4	49.0

Since this item asked specifically about paying attention to TV news concerning the presidential campaign, it is not surprising that this item is so highly related to interest in the campaign.

Use **4** or **INTEREST?** as the row variable and **11** or **READ PAPER** as the column variable and this table will appear—*press* **C** *for column percentages.*

	DAILY	WEEKLY	SELDOM
MUCH	48.4	36.5	28.1
SOMEWHAT	37.8	48.9	43.7
NOT MUCH	13.8	14.6	28.2

People who read the newspaper every day are exactly like those who watch TV news every day in terms of their level of interest.

Use **4** or **INTEREST?** as the row variable and **12** or **TALK SHOWS** as the column variable and this table will appear—*press* **C** *for column percentages.*

	YES	NO
MUCH	46.9	29.7
SOMEWHAT	40.7	46.3
NOT MUCH	12.4	24.0

Finally, people who listen to or watch talk shows are more apt to be interested in the presidential campaign.

Now, it's your turn to find out whether the media can inform as well as interest and whether the media influence voters' choices.

WORKSHEET

NAME:

COURSE:

DATE:

Workbook exercises and software are copyrighted. Copying is prohibited by law.

EXERCISE 6

1. Using the **ANES92** data set and the cross-tabulation task, create and fill in the table below. Row variable: **8** or **INFORMED?**; column variable: **9** or **TV NEWS?**. (Remember to percentage all of your tables in this exercise.)

	EVERY DAY	4–6 DAYS	2–3 DAYS	1 OR NONE
HIGH	%	%	%	%
AVERAGE	%	%	%	%
INFORMED	%	%	%	%

Prob. = _____

What is the value of Cramer's V?   V = _____

2. Create and fill in the table below. Row variable: **8** or **INFORMED?**; column variable: **10** or **TV PREZ**.

	VERY MUCH	MUCH	SOME	NOT MUCH
HIGH	%	%	%	%
AVERAGE	%	%	%	%
LOW	%	%	%	%

Prob. = _____

What is the value of Cramer's V?   V = _____

3. Create and fill in the table below. Row variable: **8** or **INFORMED?**; column variable: **11** or **READ PAPER**.

	DAILY	WEEKLY	SELDOM
HIGH	%	%	%
AVERAGE	%	%	%
LOW	%	%	%

Exercise 6: Elections and the Media

| WORKSHEET | EXERCISE 6 |

Prob. = _____

What is the value of Cramer's V? V = _____

4. Create and fill in the table below. Row variable: **8** or **INFORMED?**; column variable: **12** or **TALK SHOWS**.

	YES	NO
HIGH	%	%
AVERAGE	%	%
LOW	%	%

Prob. = _____

What is the value of Cramer's V? V = _____

Looking back over these four tables, which media variable produced the largest V with informed? _____

Which media variable produced the smallest V? _____

How would you explain this difference?

5. Create and fill in the table below. Row variable: **2** or **PRES IN 92**; column variable: **9** or **TV NEWS?**.

	EVERY DAY	4–6 DAYS	2–3 DAYS	1 OR NONE
CLINTON	%	%	%	%
BUSH	%	%	%	%
PEROT	%	%	%	%

In which group did Clinton gain the greatest support? _____

In which group did Bush gain the greatest support? _____

NAME _____   EXERCISE 6

In which group did Perot gain the greatest support? _____

Are the differences statistically significant? (circle one)   YES   NO

Prob. = _____

6. Create and fill in the table below. Row variable: **2** or **PRES IN 92**; column variable: **10** or **TV PREZ**.

	VERY MUCH	MUCH	SOME	NOT MUCH
CLINTON	%	%	%	%
BUSH	%	%	%	%
PEROT	%	%	%	%

In which group did Clinton gain the greatest support? _____

In which group did Bush gain the greatest support? _____

In which group did Perot gain the greatest support? _____

Are the differences statistically significant? (circle one)   YES   NO

Prob. = _____

7. Create and fill in the table below. Row variable: **2** or **PRES IN 92**; column variable: **11** or **READ PAPER**.

	DAILY	WEEKLY	SELDOM
CLINTON	%	%	%
BUSH	%	%	%
PEROT	%	%	%

In which group did Clinton gain the greatest support? _____

In which group did Bush gain the greatest support? _____

In which group did Perot gain the greatest support? _____

Are the differences statistically significant? (circle one)   YES   NO

Prob. = _____

Exercise 6: Elections and the Media

WORKSHEET	EXERCISE 6

8. Create and fill in the table below. Row variable: **2** or **PRES IN 92**; column variable: **12** or **TALK SHOWS**.

	YES	NO
CLINTON	%	%
BUSH	%	%
PEROT	%	%

In which group did Clinton gain the greatest support? _____

In which group did Bush gain the greatest support? _____

In which group did Perot gain the greatest support? _____

Are the differences statistically significant? (circle one)   YES   NO

Prob. = _____

9. Although significance tests greatly decrease the chances that political scientists will be fooled by random findings, a second way they guard against being fooled is to examine the same relationships in different surveys. Using the **NORC93** data set, create and fill in the table below. Row variable: **1** or **PRES IN 92**; column variable: **30** or **TV NEWS**.

	DAILY	LESS OFTEN
CLINTON	%	%
BUSH	%	%
PEROT	%	%

Are the differences statistically significant? (circle one)   YES   NO

Prob. = _____

Does this support or challenge the claim that the media influence elections? (circle one)   Supports   Challenges

NAME _____   **EXERCISE 6**

10. Create and fill in the table below. Row variable: **1** or **PRES IN 92**; column variable: **28** or **READ PAPER**.

	DAILY	WEEKLY	SELDOM
CLINTON	%	%	%
BUSH	%	%	%
PEROT	%	%	%

Are the differences statistically significant? (circle one)   YES   NO

Prob. = _____

Does this support or challenge the claim that the media influence elections? (circle one)   Supports   Challenges

11. Create and fill in the table below. Row variable: **1** or **PRES IN 92**; column variable: **31** or **TV PBS**.

	DAILY	WEEKLY	MONTHLY	RARELY
CLINTON	%	%	%	%
BUSH	%	%	%	%
PEROT	%	%	%	%

Are the differences statistically significant? (circle one)   YES   NO

Prob. = _____

Does this support or challenge the claim that the media influence elections? (circle one)   Supports   Challenges

You have examined seven tables seeking media effects on voting patterns. In how many of these tables were there significant differences?   _____

On the basis of these findings, how would you respond to someone who claimed that the news media pretty much control who gets elected president?

Exercise 6: Elections and the Media

| WORKSHEET | | | EXERCISE 6 |

12. Create and fill in the table below. Row variable: **1** or **PRES IN 92**; column variable: **56** or **PRESS?**.

	GREAT DEAL	ONLY SOME	HARDLY ANY
CLINTON	%	%	%
BUSH	%	%	%
PEROT	%	%	%

What is the long label for variable 56? (Open the F3 window to see it.)

_____

In which group did Clinton gain the greatest support?   _____

In which group did Bush gain the greatest support?   _____

In which group did Perot gain the least support?   _____

Are the differences statistically significant? (circle one)   YES   NO

Prob. = _____

Discuss the finding that how people feel about the press influences their voting patterns far more than their exposure to the media does.

PART II

PARTIES AND ISSUES

In the four exercises making up this part of the book, we are going to examine the major factors governing the political behavior of Americans: party and ideological identification and some current political issues.

◆ EXERCISE 7 ◆

Party Preference and Political Labels

Open the **NORC93** data set and go to the **Univariate Statistics** function. Use **4** or **PARTY** as the variable. This screen will appear:

Generally speaking, do you usually think of yourself as a Republican, Democrat, Independent, or what?

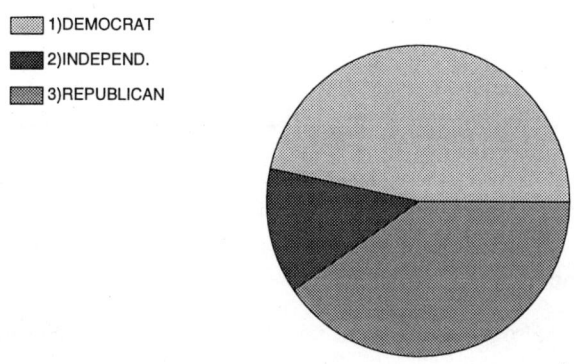

Press **D** (for Distribution). This distribution will appear:

	FREQUENCY	%
DEMOCRAT	738	46.7
INDEPENDENT	205	13.0
REPUBLICAN	637	40.3

Exercise 7: Party Preference and Political Labels

Here you can see that Democrats modestly outnumber Republicans and that most people identify with one of the two major parties—only slightly more than one in ten chose the "Independent" response. That means we can simplify the analysis of party preference by omitting the Independents and looking only at Democrats and Republicans. That is variable **85** or **DEM/REP**.

Next, use **5** or **LIB./CONS.** as the variable.

I'm going to show you a seven-point scale on which the political views that a person might hold are arranged from extremely liberal to extremely conservative. Where would you place yourself on this scale?

Persons who answered 1 through 3 were scored as liberals, those who answered 4 were scored as moderates, and those who answered 5 through 7 were scored as conservatives.

Press **D** (for Distribution). This distribution will appear:

	FREQUENCY	%
LIBERAL	413	26.7
MODERATE	575	37.1
CONSERVATIVE	560	36.2

Conservatives outnumber liberals quite substantially, as do moderates.

Select the **Tabular Statistics** function. Use **5** or **LIB./CONS.** as the row variable and use **85** or **DEM/REP** as the column variable. *Press* **C** for column percentages. This table will appear:

	DEMOCRAT	REPUBLICAN
LIBERAL	40.0	12.7
MODERATE	36.7	33.0
CONSERV.	23.3	54.3

Although the majority of Republicans regard themselves as conservative (54.3%), the majority of Democrats do not regard themselves as liberals (40.0%). This lets us see why the "L word"—liberal—has been regarded as a political liability in recent years—that candidates who are clearly identified as liberals seldom win.

Use **5** or **LIB./CONS.** as the row variable and use **8** or **RACE** as the column variable. *Press* **C** for column percentages. This table will appear:

	WHITE	AFRICAN-AM
LIBERAL	25.2	33.1
MODERATE	37.3	39.1
CONSERV.	37.2	27.8

Even the majority of African Americans do not regard themselves as liberals.

Switch to the **P1973–93** data set. This data set is based on two national surveys conducted by the National Opinion Research Center at the University of Chicago in 1973 and 1993. In fact the data for 1993 are the same as those in **NORC93**. The purpose of this data set is to permit you to compare these two years, looking for changes. Because you will find many, very substantial changes in these data, it is meaningless to examine them as a whole. That is, you will always want to use **1** or **YEAR** as the column variable. Then, to see if changes are concentrated among certain groups, you will use the appropriate variables as control variables as is demonstrated below.

Return to the **Tabular Statistics** function and use **5** or **PARTY** as the row variable and use **1** or **YEAR** as the column variable. *Press* **C** for column percentages. This table will appear:

	1973	1993
DEMOCRAT	56.3	46.7
INDEPEND.	10.0	13.0
REPUBLICAN	33.7	40.3

Here we see that during the 20-year period from 1973 to 1993 the Democratic Party lost a substantial share of political affiliation from 56.3 percent down to 46.7 percent. The difference is significant. Meanwhile, the Republicans made a substantial gain from 33.7 percent up to 40.3 percent. The percentage of Americans who claimed to be independents also rose slightly.

Next, let's see if this change in party preference applies to African Americans as well as to whites. Use **5** or **PARTY** as the row variable, use **1** or **YEAR** as the column variable, and use **2** or **RACE** as the control variable. This will create two separate tables. The first one to appear on the screen will include only white respondents. *Press* **C** for column percentages. This table will appear:

WHITE

	1973	1993
DEMOCRAT	52.5	42.0
INDEPEND.	10.5	13.2
REPUBLICAN	37.1	44.8

Among whites, the change was so substantial that in 1993 Republicans outnumbered Democrats.

Press **<ENTER>** to see the next table. *Press* **C** for column percentages. This table will appear:

AFRICAN-AM

	1973	1993
DEMOCRAT	83.7	79.9
INDEPEND.	7.0	8.0
REPUBLICAN	9.3	12.1

There is a very small drop in the percentage of Democrats among African Americans, but it is not significant.

Use **5** or **PARTY** as the row variable, use **1** or **YEAR** as the column variable, and use **3** or **REGION** as the control variable. This will create four separate tables. The first one to appear on the screen will include only people who live in the East. *Press* **C** for column percentages. This table will appear:

Exercise 7: Party Preference and Political Labels

EAST

	1973	1993
DEMOCRAT	59.1	56.4
INDEPEND.	9.9	12.9
REPUBLICAN	31.0	30.7

There was no significant change in the East.

Press <ENTER> to see the next table. *Press* **C** for column percentages. This table will appear:

MIDWEST

	1973	1993
DEMOCRAT	54.3	42.1
INDEPEND.	11.1	15.5
REPUBLICAN	34.6	42.5

There was a substantial and significant shift to the Republicans in the Midwest.

Press <ENTER> to see the next table. *Press* **C** for column percentages. This table will appear:

SOUTH

	1973	1993
DEMOCRAT	55.6	43.8
INDEPEND.	9.1	11.6
REPUBLICAN	35.3	44.6

There also was a substantial and significant shift to the Republicans in the South.

Press <ENTER> to see the next table. *Press* **C** for column percentages. This table will appear:

WEST

	1973	1993
DEMOCRAT	57.4	58.7
INDEPEND.	9.9	8.4
REPUBLICAN	32.6	32.9

Finally, there was no shift of political preferences in the West.

What about age? Perhaps not all age groups shifted affiliation.

Use **5** or **PARTY** as the row variable, use **1** or **YEAR** as the column variable, and use **4** or **AGE** as the control variable. This will create three separate tables. The first one to appear on the screen will include only people under age 30. *Press* **C** for column percentages. This table will appear:

UNDER 30

	1973	1993
DEMOCRAT	56.7	43.1
INDEPEND.	14.8	13.8
REPUBLICAN	28.5	43.1

In 1973 Democrats greatly outnumbered Republicans among young adults, but in 1993 the two parties were tied.

Press <ENTER> to see the next table. *Press* **C** for column percentages. This table will appear:

30–50

	1973	1993
DEMOCRAT	58.8	49.6
INDEPEND.	9.7	13.4
REPUBLICAN	31.5	37.1

The shift was not as dramatic among persons in the 30 to 50 age group, but it is significant.

Press <ENTER> to see the next table. *Press* **C** for column percentages. This table will appear:

50 & OVER

	1973	1993
DEMOCRAT	54.0	45.4
INDEPEND.	7.2	11.9
REPUBLICAN	38.8	42.8

Even among older Americans, the Democrats declined while the Republicans rose and the differences are significant.

So, now you know how to analyze these data to discover changes. The major use of this data set will be for some of the *Optional Challenge Questions* which begin with Exercise 13. Whether or not these challenge questions are part of your regular assignment, will serve as a basis for additional credit, or are simply for your own amusement will be up to your instructor. They were written to allow you considerable freedom to follow your own hunches, and that's why they do not begin until you have had a lot of experience.

WORKSHEET

NAME:

COURSE:

DATE:

EXERCISE 7

Workbook exercises and software are copyrighted. Copying is prohibited by law.

1. Open the **NORC93** data set and create and fill in the table below. Row variable: **85** or **DEM/REP**; column variable: **8** or **RACE**. (Remember to percentage your tables.)

	WHITE	AFRICAN-AM
DEMOCRAT	%	%
REPUBLICAN	%	%

Are whites or African Americans more likely to be Democrats? _____

2. Create and fill in the table below. Row variable: **85** or **DEM/REP**; column variable: **23** or **REGION**.

	EAST	MIDWEST	SOUTH	WEST
DEMOCRAT	%	%	%	%
REPUBLICAN	%	%	%	%

In which regions are the Democrats strongest? _____ _____

In which regions are the Republicans strongest? _____ _____

Prob. = _____

What is the value of Cramer's V?   V = _____

Now create this same table, but use the subset feature to limit the table to whites. (Enter **8** or **RACE** as the subset variable and select **1** as both the lower and upper limits.)

SUBSET WITH VALUE WHITE

	EAST	MIDWEST	SOUTH	WEST
DEMOCRAT	%	%	%	%
REPUBLICAN	%	%	%	%

Prob. = _____

Exercise 7: Party Preference and Political Labels   67

| WORKSHEET | EXERCISE 7 |

What is the value of Cramer's V?   V = _____

Is the correlation higher or lower when
only whites are examined? (circle one)   HIGHER   LOWER

3. Create and fill in the table below. Row variable: **85** or **DEM/REP**; column variable: **12** or **RELIGION**.

	CATHOLIC	LIB PROT	CONS PROT	JEW	NONE
DEMOCRAT	%	%	%	%	%
REPUBLICAN	%	%	%	%	%

Among whom are the Democrats strongest?   _____

Among whom are the Republicans strongest?   _____

Prob. = _____

What is the value of Cramer's V?   V = _____

Now create this same table, but use the subset feature to limit the table to whites. Use **85** or **DEM/REP** as the row variable; *however*, because of lack of cases of Jews and Nones, use variable **86** or **CATH/PROT** as the column variable.

	CATHOLIC	LIB.PROT	CONS.PROT
DEMOCRAT	%	%	%
REPUBLICAN	%	%	%

Among whom are the Democrats strongest?   _____

Among whom are the Republicans strongest?   _____

Prob. = _____

What is the value of Cramer's V?   V = _____

Which religious group is changed the most when only
whites are examined?   _____

NAME _____   EXERCISE 7

4. Create and fill in the table below. Row variable: **85** or **DEM/REP**; column variable: **18** or **FAMILY $**.

	UNDER $12K	$12–$23K	$23–$35K	$35–$60K	OVER $60K
DEMOCRAT	%	%	%	%	%
REPUBLICAN	%	%	%	%	%

In which income group are the Democrats strongest? _____

In which income group are the Republicans strongest? _____

Prob. = _____

What is the value of Cramer's V? V = _____

Now create this same table, but use the subset feature to limit the table to whites.

SUBSET WITH VALUE WHITE

	UNDER $12K	$12–$23K	$23–$35K	$35–$60K	OVER $60K
DEMOCRAT	%	%	%	%	%
REPUBLICAN	%	%	%	%	%

Prob. = _____

What is the value of Cramer's V? V = _____

Is the correlation higher, lower, or about the same when only whites are examined? (circle one)   HIGHER   LOWER   SAME

5. Create and fill in the table below. Row variable: **85** or **DEM/REP**; column variable: **7** or **AGE**.

	18–29	30–39	40–49	50–65	OVER 65
DEMOCRAT	%	%	%	%	%
REPUBLICAN	%	%	%	%	%

Among whom are the Democrats strongest? _____

Among whom are the Republicans strongest? _____

Is the difference statistically significant? (circle one)   YES   NO

Prob. = _____

Exercise 7: Party Preference and Political Labels

WORKSHEET	EXERCISE 7

What is the value of Cramer's V? V = _____

6. Create and fill in the table below. Row variable: **85** or **DEM/REP**; column variable: **6** or **SEX**.

	MALE	FEMALE
DEMOCRAT	%	%
REPUBLICAN	%	%

Among whom are the Republicans stronger? _____

Prob. = _____

What is the value of Cramer's V? V = _____

7. Create and fill in the table below. Row variable: **85** or **DEM/REP**; column variable: **29** or **WATCH TV**.

	1 OR LESS	TWO	3–4	OVER 4
DEMOCRAT	%	%	%	%
REPUBLICAN	%	%	%	%

Among whom are the Republicans strongest? _____

Is the difference statistically significant? (circle one)   YES   NO

Prob. = _____

What is the value of Cramer's V? V = _____

8. Based on all these results, create a profile of the kind of person who is most apt to say that he or she is a Republican. Then do the same thing for the kind of person who is most apt to say that she or he is a Democrat.

   A person with the following characteristics is most apt to be a:

   REPUBLICAN   DEMOCRAT

◆ EXERCISE 8 ◆
The Tax Issue

Open the **NORC93** data set and go to the **Univariate Statistics** function. Use **49** or **TAX 2 HIGH** as the variable. *Press <ENTER>* to pass through the subset option. This screen will appear:

Do you consider the amount of federal income tax which you have to pay as too high, about right, or too low?

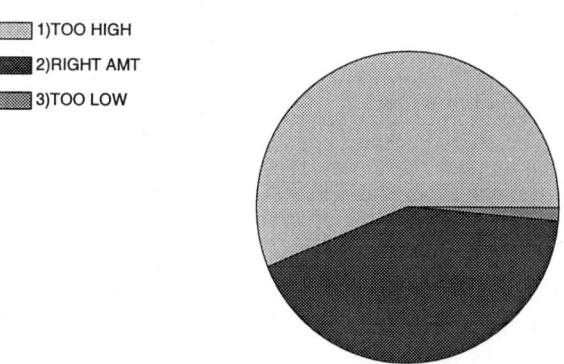

Press **D** (for Distribution). This distribution will appear:

	FREQUENCY	%
TOO HIGH	582	56.5
RIGHT AMT	436	42.3
TOO LOW	13	1.3

Most Americans think their taxes are too high. Virtually no one (only 13 people) thought their taxes were too low. To make the analysis more efficient we will simply eliminate those 13 people and use variable **87** or **OVER TAXED** as the basis for this exercise. Now let's find out if various kinds of people differ in their views of income taxes.

Select the **Tabular Statistics** function. Use **87** or **OVER TAXED** as the row variable and use **6** or **SEX** as the column variable. *Press* **C** for column percentages. This table will appear:

	MALE	FEMALE
TOO HIGH	58.4	56.2
ABOUT RITE[1]	41.6	43.8

There is a tiny difference between men and women, but if you *press* **S** (for statistics) you will discover that it is not significant.

---

[1] Since MicroCase limits variable names and categories to 10 characters, some variable information is purposely shortened or misspelled. To be consistent with the software, the same spelling is generally used in the text whenever variable names and categories are referred to. (Of course, the proper spelling for "rite" is "right.")

Use **87** or **OVER TAXED** as the row variable and use **5** or **LIB./CONS.** as the column variable. *Press* **C** for column percentages. This table will appear:

	LIBERAL	MODERATE	CONSERV.
TOO HIGH	47.5	58.6	62.9
ABOUT RITE	52.5	41.4	37.1

No surprise here—liberals are less likely to think their taxes are too high, although even among them nearly half do, while the majority of moderates and conservatives think their taxes are too high.

Use **87** or **OVER TAXED** as the row variable and use **1** or **PRES IN 92** as the column variable. *Press* **C** for column percentages. This table will appear:

	CLINTON	BUSH	PEROT
TOO HIGH	51.5	58.9	63.0
ABOUT RITE	48.5	41.1	37.0

Americans who voted for Clinton were a bit less likely than those who voted for Bush to think their taxes were too high. Perot voters were most likely to object to their taxes.

Use **87** or **OVER TAXED** as the row variable and use **20** or **UNIONIZED?** as the column variable. *Press* **C** for column percentages. This table will appear:

	UNIONIZED	NOT UNIONIZED
TOO HIGH	63.4	56.2
ABOUT RITE	36.6	43.8

Perhaps this is a surprise—union members are more likely than others to think their taxes are too high. However, the difference is not significant.

Now, it's your turn.

WORKSHEET

NAME:

COURSE:

DATE:

Workbook exercises and software are copyrighted. Copying is prohibited by law.

EXERCISE 8

1. Using the **NORC93** data set, create and fill in the table below. Row variable: **87** or **OVER TAXED**; column variable: **8** or **RACE**. (Remember to percentage all of your tables.)

	WHITES	AFRICAN-AM
TOO HIGH	%	%
ABOUT RITE	%	%

Are African Americans or whites more likely to think their taxes are too high? _____

Is the difference significant? (circle one)   YES   NO

Prob. = _____

What is the value of Cramer's V?   V = _____

2. Create and fill in the table below. Row variable: **87** or **OVER TAXED**; column variable: **85** or **DEM/REP**.

	DEMOCRAT	REPUBLICAN
TOO HIGH	%	%
ABOUT RITE	%	%

Are Democrats or Republicans more likely to think their taxes are too high? _____

Is the difference significant? (circle one)   YES   NO

Prob. = _____

What is the value of Cramer's V?   V = _____

Exercise 8: The Tax Issue

WORKSHEET

EXERCISE 8

3. Create and fill in this same table, but use the subset function to limit the data to whites. (Enter **8** or **RACE** as the subset variable and select **1** as both the lower and upper limits.)

SUBSET WITH VALUE WHITE

	DEMOCRAT	REPUBLICAN
TOO HIGH	%	%
ABOUT RITE	%	%

Prob. = _____

What is the value of Cramer's V?   V = _____

Is the correlation higher, lower, or about the same when only whites are examined? (circle one)   HIGHER   LOWER   SAME

4. Create and fill in the table below. Row variable: **87** or **OVER TAXED**; column variable: **23** or **REGION**.

	EAST	MIDWEST	SOUTH	WEST
TOO HIGH	%	%	%	%
ABOUT RITE	%	%	%	%

In which region are people most apt to think their taxes are too high? _____

In which region are people least apt to think their taxes are too high? _____

Is the difference significant? (circle one)   YES   NO

Prob. = _____

What is the value of Cramer's V?   V = _____

5. Create and fill in the table below. Row variable: **87** or **OVER TAXED**; column variable: **9** or **MARITAL**.

	MARRIED	DIV/SEP	WIDOWED	SINGLE
TOO HIGH	%	%	%	%
ABOUT RITE	%	%	%	%

NAME	EXERCISE 8

Are these differences significant? (circle one)   YES   NO

Prob. = _____

What is the value of Cramer's V?   V = _____

6. Create and fill in the table below. Row variable: **87** or **OVER TAXED**; column variable: **7** or **AGE**.

	18–29	30–39	40–49	50–65	OVER 65
TOO HIGH	%	%	%	%	%
ABOUT RITE	%	%	%	%	%

Which age group is most apt to think their taxes are about right? _____

Which age group is the next most likely to think their taxes are about right? _____

Are these differences significant? (circle one)   YES   NO

Prob. = _____

What is the value of Cramer's V?   V = _____

What do you think these two age groups have in common that might cause them to differ in this way from other age groups?

7. Create and fill in the table below. Row variable: **87** or **OVER TAXED**; column variable: **33** or **COUNTRY&W**.

	LIKES	MIXED	DISLIKES
TOO HIGH	%	%	%
ABOUT RITE	%	%	%

Exercise 8: The Tax Issue

WORKSHEET	EXERCISE 8

Are these differences significant? (circle one)   YES   NO

Prob. = _____

What is the value of Cramer's V?   V = _____

How would you explain this finding?

8. Create and fill in the table below. Row variable: **87** or **OVER TAXED**; column variable: **16** or **OCC. PREST**.

	LOW	MED LOW	MED HIGH	HIGH
TOO HIGH	%	%	%	%
ABOUT RITE	%	%	%	%

Are people in the highest-status occupations more or less likely than people in the lowest-status occupations to think their taxes are too high? (circle one)   MORE   LESS

Is the difference significant? (circle one)   YES   NO

Prob. = _____

What is the value of Cramer's V?   V = _____

Does this finding agree or disagree with what you expected? Elaborate.

♦ EXERCISE 9 ♦
The Issue of Entitlements

Today, many political discussions focus on "entitlements." Entitlements are benefits paid to individuals qualified by law to receive them—hence those who receive them are legally entitled to them. Because entitlements rapidly are becoming the major government expense, all plans to cut budgets or to reduce the debt must consider how entitlements could be reduced. Of course, those receiving such benefits tend to search for candidates who promise to protect their entitlement. To get some sense of the role played by entitlements in current political processes, let's see how many people are getting what, and how this was reflected in their 1992 voting.

Open the **ANES92** data set and go to the **Univariate Statistics** function. Use **13** or **ON SOC SEC** as the variable. *Press* <ENTER> to skip the subset section. This screen will appear:

SOCIAL SECURITY RECIPIENT?

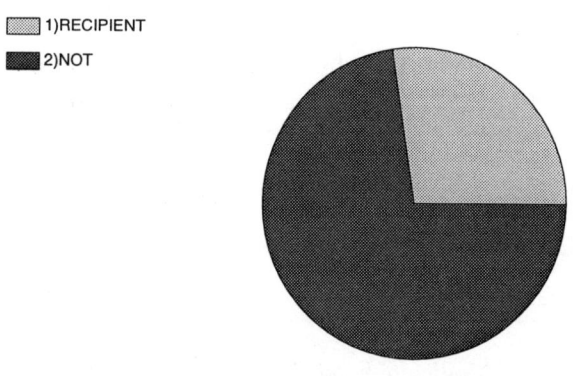

Press **D** (for Distribution). This distribution will appear:

	FREQUENCY	%
RECIPIENT	679	27.4
NOT	1797	72.6

More than 1 person in 4 said they currently received social security benefits. Because for many years Congress treated the money people paid into social security as income and spent it as it came in, they failed to build up a social security trust fund from which to pay these benefits. Consequently, current social security payments are funded by current contributions so that those who retire must be supported by those still working. The trouble is that current population trends will soon result in more people being old enough to qualify for social security than are still working. Clearly, eventually some people will have to be denied social security benefits or at least to have their benefits greatly reduced. However, as older people become a larger percentage of the population they also become a larger proportion of voters. And that makes it increasingly politically difficult to reduce benefits that people have been promised their entire working lives and for which they already have paid very substantial amounts.

Exercise 9: The Issue of Entitlements

In addition to social security payments, many retired people also are eligible for Medicare. Use **15** or **MEDICARE?** as the variable. *Press* **D** (for Distribution). This distribution will appear:

	FREQUENCY	%
RECIPIENT	558	22.5
NOT	1920	77.5

The unemployed also are eligible for government payments for a number of months as they seek new jobs. Use **17** or **ON UNEMPL.** as the variable. *Press* **D** (for Distribution). This distribution will appear:

	FREQUENCY	%
RECIPIENT	110	4.4
NOT	2366	95.6

At the time this survey was taken, just after the 1992 election, 4.4 percent reported they were receiving unemployment benefits.

Other entitlements come under the general heading of welfare. Medicaid provides health care for persons whose income is sufficiently low so that they qualify. Use **16** or **MEDICAID?** as the variable. *Press* **D** (for Distribution). This distribution will appear:

	FREQUENCY	%
RECIPIENT	261	10.6
NOT	2205	89.4

Ten percent reported receiving Medicaid. Food stamps are another benefit for low-income people. Use **14** or **FD. STAMPS** as the variable. *Press* **D** (for Distribution). This distribution will appear:

	FREQUENCY	%
RECIPIENT	227	9.2
NOT	2252	90.8

When most people speak of welfare they mean the program known as Aid to Families with Dependent Children, or AFDC. This program was begun to allow women without husbands to stay at home with their children rather than go out to work or to put the children in foster homes. Use **18** or **ON AFDC?** as the variable. *Press* **D** (for Distribution). This distribution will appear:

	FREQUENCY	%
RECIPIENT	95	3.8
NOT	2378	96.2

In this sample about 4 percent of the respondents were currently receiving AFDC payments.

Did people vote to protect their entitlements in 1992?

Select the **Tabular Statistics** function. Use **2** or **PRES IN 92** as the row variable and use **13** or **ON SOC SEC** as the column variable. *Press* **C** for column percentages. This table will appear:

	RECIPIENT	NOT
CLINTON	52.5	46.0
BUSH	33.7	34.1
PEROT	13.7	19.9

The differences are significant, but they are small. There was not a very strong tendency for persons on social security to flock to Clinton.

Use **2** or **PRES IN 92** as the row variable and use **17** or **ON UNEMPL.** as the column variable. *Press* **C** for column percentages. This table will appear:

	RECIPIENT	NOT
CLINTON	49.3	47.7
BUSH	23.9	34.5
PEROT	26.9	17.8

Here the differences are not significant—unemployed people were not more likely to have voted for Clinton. However, the lack of significance also reflects the small number of unemployed persons (67) on whom the percentages are based.

Use **2** or **PRES IN 92** as the row variable and use **14** or **FD. STAMPS** as the column variable. *Press* **C** for column percentages. This table will appear:

	RECIPIENT	NOT
CLINTON	70.8	46.6
BUSH	22.5	34.6
PEROT	6.7	18.8

But here the effects are very strong. People on food stamps voted overwhelmingly for Clinton. Notice how poorly Perot did among them too.

These data suggest that welfare entitlements had a substantial effect on voting, but that social security and unemployment entitlements had little or no effect. Now let's see how American voters feel about welfare and whether this influenced how they voted. Open the **NORC93** data set and go to the **Univariate Statistics** function. Use **88** or **WELFARE $** as the variable. *Press* **D** (for Distribution). This distribution will appear:

What about the current level of spending on welfare?

	FREQUENCY	%
TOO LITTLE	130	17.2
ABOUT RITE	198	26.2
TOO MUCH	428	56.6

Exercise 9: The Issue of Entitlements

Clearly, most Americans are opposed to current levels of spending for welfare. But does this mean that they lack sympathy for the poor? Use **89** or **POOR $** as the variable. The screen asks whether you wish a bar graph or a pie chart. *Press* **2** for pie chart. *Press* **D** (for Distribution). This distribution will appear:

What about current levels of spending on assistance to the poor?

	FREQUENCY	%
TOO LITTLE	497	64.6
ABOUT RITE	177	23.0
TOO MUCH	95	12.4

A dramatic difference. The majority of Americans think too little is spent on assistance to the poor. Obviously, they think welfare fails to accomplish that goal. Results like this remind us that it is very important to know just how political pollsters word their questions. In fact, the political implications of these two findings are rather different, as you now will discover.

WORKSHEET

NAME:

COURSE:

DATE:

Workbook exercises and software are copyrighted. Copying is prohibited by law.

EXERCISE 9

1. Using the **NORC93** data set, go to the **Tabular Statistics** function and create and fill in the table below. Row variable: **1** or **PRES IN 92**; column variable: **88** or **WELFARE $**. (Be sure to percentage the tables.)

	TOO LITTLE	ABOUT RITE	TOO MUCH
CLINTON	%	%	%
BUSH	%	%	%
PEROT	%	%	%

Which group gave the highest percentage of their votes to Clinton? _____

Which group gave the highest percentage of their votes to Bush? _____

Are these differences significant? (circle one)   YES   NO

Prob. = _____

What is the value of Cramer's V?   V = _____

2. Create and fill in the table below. Row variable: **1** or **PRES IN 92**; column variable: **89** or **POOR $**.

	TOO LITTLE	ABOUT RITE	TOO MUCH
CLINTON	%	%	%
BUSH	%	%	%
PEROT	%	%	%

Which group gave the highest percentage of their votes to Clinton? _____

Which group gave the highest percentage of their votes to Bush? _____

Are these differences significant? (circle one)   YES   NO

Exercise 9: The Issue of Entitlements

| WORKSHEET | EXERCISE 9 |

Prob. = _____

What is the value of Cramer's V?   V = _____

Based on these results, evaluate this campaign slogan: Let's spend less on welfare and spend more to help the poor.

3. Create and fill in the table below. Row variable: **88** or **WELFARE $**; column variable: **8** or **RACE**.

	WHITE	AFRICAN-AM
TOO LITTLE	%	%
ABOUT RITE	%	%
TOO MUCH	%	%

Do most African Americans think too little is spent on welfare? (circle one)   YES   NO

Are these differences significant? (circle one)   YES   NO

Prob. = _____

What is the value of Cramer's V?   V = _____

4. Create and fill in the table below. Row variable: **89** or **POOR $**; column variable: **8** or **RACE**.

	WHITE	AFRICAN-AM
TOO LITTLE	%	%
ABOUT RITE	%	%
TOO MUCH	%	%

Do most white Americans think too much is spent on the poor? (circle one)   YES   NO

Part II: Parties and Issues

NAME _____ EXERCISE 9

Are these differences significant? (circle one)   YES   NO

Prob. = _____

What is the value of Cramer's V?   V = _____

Do the results in these two tables support or challenge the impression about the relationship between race and attitudes about welfare you have gained from the news media? Explain.

5. Create and fill in the table below. Row variable: **88** or **WELFARE $**; column variable: **85** or **DEM/REP**.

	DEMOCRAT	REPUBLICAN
TOO LITTLE	%	%
ABOUT RITE	%	%
TOO MUCH	%	%

Do most Democrats think too little is spent on welfare? (circle one)   YES   NO

Are these differences significant? (circle one)   YES   NO

Prob. = _____

What is the value of Cramer's V?   V = _____

6. Create and fill in the table below. Row variable: **89** or **POOR $**; column variable: **85** or **DEM/REP**.

	DEMOCRAT	REPUBLICAN
TOO LITTLE	%	%
ABOUT RITE	%	%
TOO MUCH	%	%

Exercise 9: The Issue of Entitlements

WORKSHEET	EXERCISE 9

Do most Republicans think too much is spent on the poor? (circle one)   YES   NO

Are these differences significant? (circle one)   YES   NO

Prob. = _____

What is the value of Cramer's V?   V = _____

Do the results in these two tables support or challenge the impression about the relationship between party affiliation and attitudes about welfare you have gained from the news media? Explain.

◆ EXERCISE 10 ◆
The Abortion Issue

Recently, abortion has become a very major issue in American politics. In this assignment you are first going to examine the social geography of the actual abortion rate, state by state. Then you will use the survey data to examine attitudes about abortion.

Once again open the **FIFTY** data file and go to the mapping function. This time create the map for variable **43** or **ABORTION**. This map of the abortion rate will appear on your screen:

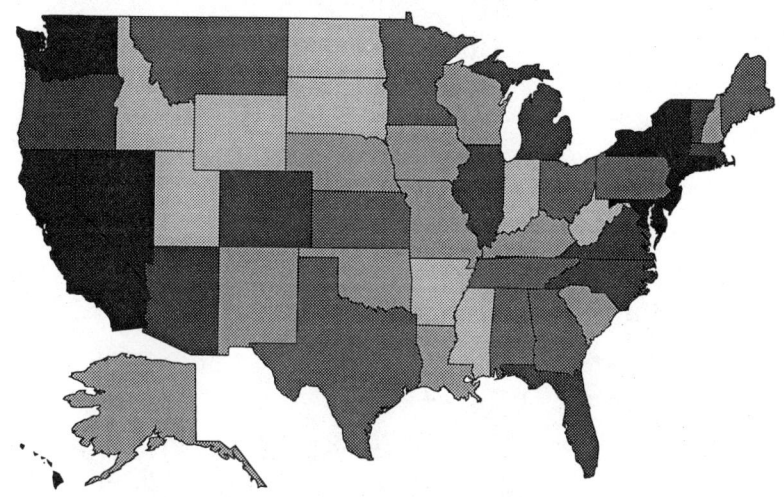

1988: Abortions per 1,000 live births

There are many ways such a rate could be computed. The number of abortions per year could be divided by the total population and the result multiplied by 1,000 thus creating a rate of abortions per 1,000 population. But this would create problems since only pregnant women can have abortions and states will differ in their proportions of women in their child-bearing years. So the Bureau of Health Statistics calculates the abortion rate based on the number of abortions per 1,000 live births.

Press **N** (for Name) to see which state was highest.

New York changes color and you can see that it has a rate of 634 abortions for every 1,000 live births. Put another way, at least 38.8 percent of pregnancies in New York are terminated by abortion. *Press* the **down arrow** to see the next highest state. California is second with a rate of 598. Hawaii is third highest with a rate of 579. Now *press* **D** (for Distribution) to see all 50 states ranked from high to low. Looking at the list you can see that Nevada and New Jersey are in fourth and fifth place, followed by Connecticut.

This mixture of East and West Coast states reflects the fact that high abortion rates are a bi-coastal phenomenon—the bottom of the list is dominated by Southern and inland states. That is, the abortion rate is highest in the highly urban states where most people live in major metropolitan areas.

To see this, map **56** or **% METROPOL**.

Notice how very similar this map is to the map of abortions.

Exercise 10: The Abortion Issue

What is it about life in large cities that may sustain a high abortion rate? One possibility is that the culture of large cities encourages sexual activity among unmarried persons and sustains a climate of cosmopolitan or "sophisticated" opinion favorable to abortion. How could we test this hypothesis? How about wine consumption? Map variable **67** or **% WINE**—the proportion of alcoholic beverages consumed in a state that is wine.

Notice how very similar this map is to the map of abortions and to the map of the percent living in metropolitan areas.

Now *press* **D** (for Distribution) to see all 50 states ranked from high to low wine consumption. Looking at the list you can see that California and Colorado are highest, followed by New Jersey, Connecticut, Washington, and New York. This too is like the distribution of the abortion rate.

For the remainder of this analysis of data on the states you can use **43** or **ABORTION** as the initial map and use the compare map function to generate the series of comparisons outlined below. Notice that when you use the compare map function the correlation coefficient appears in the upper right corner of the screen (r =). When the correlation is followed by 1 asterisk (*) it is significant beyond the 0.05 level. Two asterisks (**) indicate significance beyond the .01 level. Correlations without asterisks are not significant.

Those of you *not* having VGA graphics (and hence do not have available the compare map function) should produce the results below by using the scatterplot function.

Use **43** or **ABORTION** as the dependent variable and **67** or **% WINE** as the independent variable. The correlation is huge (r = 0.76) and extremely significant (Prob. = 0.000).

Next, use **43** or **ABORTION** as the dependent variable and use **48** or **GOURMET** as the independent variable. Here we see that the circulation of *Gourmet Magazine*, another measure of "sophistication," also is highly correlated with the abortion rate (r = 0.69).

Use **43** or **ABORTION** as the dependent variable and use **69** or **COSMO** as the independent variable. Here we see that the circulation of *Cosmopolitan Magazine*, another measure of "sophistication," also is highly correlated with the abortion rate (r = 0.68).

Now, use **43** or **ABORTION** as the dependent variable and use **46** or **FLD&STREAM** as the independent variable. Here we see that the circulation of *Field & Stream Magazine*, quite the opposite of a measure of "sophistication," is highly **negatively** correlated with the abortion rate (r = –0.73).

As a contrast to the findings about wine consumption, use **43** or **ABORTION** as the dependent variable and use **68** or **%BEER** as the independent variable. Another very strong **negative** correlation (r = –0.73).

As another measure of non-cosmopolitan culture, use **43** or **ABORTION** as the dependent variable and **45** or **PICKUPS** as the independent variable. Here we see that where pickup trucks are popular the abortion rate tends to be low (r = –0.68).

To continue, use **43** or **ABORTION** as the dependent variable and use **71** or **SHRINKS** as the independent variable. Here we see that there is a strong, positive correlation between the abortion rate and the number of psychiatrists per 100,000 population (r = 0.66).

Now try **43** or **ABORTION** as the dependent variable and use **63** or **% SINGLES** as the independent variable. This results in a huge, **positive** correlation between the abortion rate and the proportion of the population made up of single adults (r = 0.63).

Try **43** or **ABORTION** as the dependent variable and use **8** or **%CLINTON92** as the independent variable. Since Clinton made a campaign promise to appoint a "pro-choice" judge to the Supreme Court, it is perhaps not surprising that there is a modest correlation between the abortion rate and the percent who voted for President Clinton (r = 0.46). It also is significant.

In the exercise that follows, you will be asked to check out the findings based on aggregate data for states with survey data on individuals. But first, let's examine several questions about abortion from among the several available in the survey.

Open the **NORC93** data set and go to the **Univariate Statistics** function. Use **65** or **MOM HEALTH** as the variable. When the pie chart appears, *press* **D** (for Distribution). This distribution will appear:

LEGAL ABORTION: If the woman's own health is seriously endangered by the pregnancy?

	FREQUENCY	%
APPROVE	923	89.8
DISAPPROVE	105	10.2

This question is one of a series directed toward whether or not the respondent would approve or disapprove of abortion being legal in various circumstances. Notice that respondents aren't just saying they personally approve or disapprove of abortion under these various circumstances, but whether they approve or disapprove of abortion being *legal* under these circumstances. The overwhelming majority of Americans approve of abortion to protect a woman's health.

Use **63** or **DEFECT** as the variable.

LEGAL ABORTION: If there is a strong chance of serious defect in the baby?

	FREQUENCY	%
APPROVE	840	81.3
DISAPPROVE	193	18.7

Again there is a very high level of approval, but a bit lower than when the mother's health is at stake.

Next, use **64** or **UNWANTED** as the variable.

LEGAL ABORTION: If she is married and does not want any more children?

	FREQUENCY	%
APPROVE	480	47.1
DISAPPROVE	539	52.9

Now, try **66** or **UNWED** as the variable.

Exercise 10: The Abortion Issue

LEGAL ABORTION: If she is not married and does not want to marry the man?

	FREQUENCY	%
APPROVE	488	48.1
DISAPPROVE	526	51.9

It's nearly identical to the previous result. Finally, try **67** or **ABORTION** as the variable.

LEGAL ABORTION: If the woman wants it for any reason?

	FREQUENCY	%
APPROVE	458	45.3
DISAPPROVE	552	54.7

As we can see on these last three questions, however, solid and consistent majorities disapprove of abortion when it is a matter of convenience or pure choice.

Variable **67** or **ABORTION** seems the most general measure of the five and will be the basis for the analysis that follows. Please feel free to try the exercises with some of these other measures as well.

Your turn.

WORKSHEET

NAME:

COURSE:

DATE:

EXERCISE 10

Workbook exercises and software are copyrighted. Copying is prohibited by law.

1. Using the **NORC93** data set and the **Tabular Statistics** function, create and fill in the table below. Row variable: **67** or **ABORTION**; column variable: **6** or **SEX**. (Make sure to use column percentaging for each table in this exercise.)

	MALE	FEMALE
APPROVE	%	%
DISAPPROVE	%	%

   Is the result significant? (circle one)   YES   NO

   Prob. = _____

   What is the value of Cramer's V?   V = _____

2. Create and fill in the table below. Row variable: **67** or **ABORTION**; column variable: **10** or **#CHILDREN**.

	NONE	ONE	TWO	3 OR MORE
APPROVE	%	%	%	%
DISAPPROVE	%	%	%	%

   In which group is there the least support for abortion? _____

   Is the result significant? (circle one)   YES   NO

   Prob. = _____

   What is the value of Cramer's V?   V = _____

3. Create and fill in the table below. Row variable: **67** or **ABORTION**; column variable: **9** or **MARITAL**.

	MARRIED	DIV/SEP	WIDOWED	SINGLE
APPROVE	%	%	%	%
DISAPPROVE	%	%	%	%

Exercise 10: The Abortion Issue

WORKSHEET	EXERCISE 10

In which group is there the least support for abortion? _____

In which group is there the most support for abortion? _____

Is the result significant? (circle one)   YES   NO

Prob. = _____

What is the value of Cramer's V?   V = _____

*Referring to the findings based on the **FIFTY** data set, do the survey data give essentially the same results in this instance? (circle one)*   YES   NO

4. Create and fill in the table below. Row variable: **67** or **ABORTION**; column variable: **8** or **RACE**.

	WHITE	AFRICAN-AM
APPROVE	%	%
DISAPPROVE	%	%

Is the result significant? (circle one)   YES   NO

Prob. = _____

What is the value of Cramer's V?   V = _____

5. Create and fill in the table below. Row variable: **67** or **ABORTION**; column variable: **7** or **AGE**.

	18–29	30–39	40–49	50–65	OVER 65
APPROVE	%	%	%	%	%
DISAPPROVE	%	%	%	%	%

In which age group is there the least support for abortion? _____

In which age group is there the most support for abortion? _____

Is the result significant? (circle one)   YES   NO

Prob. = _____

What is the value of Cramer's V?   V = _____

NAME _____   **EXERCISE 10**

6. Create and fill in the table below. Row variable: **67** or **ABORTION**; column variable: **85** or **DEM/REP**.

	DEMOCRAT	REPUBLICAN
APPROVE	%	%
DISAPPROVE	%	%

Is the result significant? (circle one)   YES   NO

Prob. = _____

What is the value of Cramer's V?   V = _____

7. Create and fill in the table below. Row variable: **1** or **PRES IN 92**; column variable: **67** or **ABORTION**.

	APPROVE	DISAPPROVE
CLINTON	%	%
BUSH	%	%
PEROT	%	%

Who was the winner among those who approve of abortion for any reason the woman wishes?   _____

Who was the winner among those who disapprove of abortion for any reason the woman wishes?   _____

Is the result significant? (circle one)   YES   NO

Prob. = _____

What is the value of Cramer's V?   V = _____

Referring to the findings based on the **FIFTY** data set, do the survey data give essentially the same results in this instance? (circle one)   YES   NO

Exercise 10: The Abortion Issue

WORKSHEET — EXERCISE 10

8. Create and fill in the table below. Row variable: **67** or **ABORTION**; column variable: **12** or **RELIGION**.

	CATHOLIC	LIB PROT	CONS PROT	JEW	NONE
APPROVE	%	%	%	%	%
DISAPPROVE	%	%	%	%	%

In which group is there the least support for abortion? _____

In which group is there the most support for abortion? _____

Are these results significant? (circle one)   YES   NO

Prob. = _____

What is the value of Cramer's V?   V = _____

9. Assume that people who disapprove of abortions for any reason are "pro-life" and those who approve are "pro-choice." Create a profile of the kinds of people who are apt to be pro-life; then do the same for pro-choice. I have listed one characteristic of each to help you get started.

PRO-LIFE   PRO-CHOICE
Widowed   Single

PART III

INSTITUTIONS OF GOVERNMENT

In the following five exercises you will explore the three branches of government—the legislative, the executive, and the judicial. Primary emphasis will be on Congress using two data sets, one consisting of all 435 members of the House and the other all 100 senators of the 104th Congress, which convened in January 1995.

◆ EXERCISE 11 ◆

Who's in the House and Senate?

Open the **HOUSE** data file and go to the **Univariate Statistics** function and *press <ENTER>*. Use **2** or **STATE** as the variable. When the screen asks for a subset variable, simply *press <ENTER>* to continue. A bar graph appears on the screen.

The arrow is under the first vertical bar. This bar represents Alabama, and you can see that 7 members of the U.S. House of Representatives are from that state. Use the **right arrow** key to place the arrow under the next bar. This bar is for Alaska, and Alaska has but one representative. *Press* **T** (for Table). Now you can see how many representatives each state had in the 104th Congress. California is highest with 52. New York is next with 31, just barely ahead of Texas with 30. Membership in the House is based on population, so the more populous states have the most members. As states undergo different rates of growth or decline and their populations change relative to one another, their numbers of seats are reapportioned. Reapportionment takes place the year after the census and goes into effect during the next election. For example, during the 1980s California had only 45 seats, New York had 34, and Texas 27. Following the returns from the 1990 census, seats were reapportioned to reflect population changes. Therefore, the 103rd Congress (elected in 1992) was reapportioned giving California and Texas (and several other states) more seats in the House, while reducing New York's seats from 34 to 30. However, no state, no matter how small, may be denied at least one representative. Notice that many states do have only one. Since each state has two senators, that means states such as North and South Dakota have twice as many senators as they do members of the House.

Now, let's break the House down by region. Use **3** or **REGION** as the variable. After you have examined the pie chart, *Press* **D** (for Distribution).

	FREQUENCY	%
EAST	88	20.2
MIDWEST	105	24.1
SOUTH	149	34.3
WEST	93	21.4

Since the South includes the largest number of states of any region, it is no surprise that it has the largest number of members of the House. And since the population in the South is growing, its total number of seats increased by 7 following the 1990 Census. The Midwest region has the second largest bloc of seats (105), but lost 8 seats during the recent reapportionment. The East also lost seats, while western seats increased from 85 to 93.

Now, let's break the House down by party. Use **9** or **PARTY** as the variable. When the pie chart appears, *press* **D** (for Distribution).

	FREQUENCY	%
DEMOCRAT	204	47.0
REPUBLICAN	230	53.0

Until the 1994 election, Democrats had outnumbered Republicans in Congress for forty years and before the 1994 election had controlled the House by a margin of about three to two, a decline from their margin of nearly two to one in the previous session of Congress. The 1994 election resulted in a huge shift of power. Now Republicans outnumber Democrats by 230 to 204. *Press* **T** (for Table). Notice that there is missing data on one case. This is Bernard Sanders of Vermont, who was elected to Congress as an independent and who identifies himself as a socialist. Because of Sanders, when you examine votes by party, the total vote will always be one short of the full House membership. To obtain the accurate total vote, use the **Univariate Statistics** function.

Use **12** or **SEX** as the variable. *Press* **D** (for Distribution).

	FREQUENCY	%
MALE	388	89.2
FEMALE	47	10.8

There are not many women in the House—only 47 out of 435 U.S. representatives are women. This is exactly the same number as in the previous Congress.

Use **11** or **AGE** as the variable. *Press* **D** (for Distribution).

	FREQUENCY	%
45 OR LESS	120	28.0
46–55	162	37.8
56–65	102	23.8
OVER 65	45	10.5

Only persons 25 and over are eligible to serve in the House. The 104th Congress is younger than the 103rd, with 120 members under 45 (compared with 101). Still, most representatives are over 45.

Use **14** or **MARITAL** as the variable. *Press* **D** (for Distribution).

	FREQUENCY	%
MARRIED	364	83.7
DIV/SEP	31	7.1
SINGLE	32	7.4
WIDOWED	8	1.8

The overwhelming majority of U.S. representatives are married. However, the number who are single increased from 28 to 32 since the 103rd Congress.

Use **13** or **EDUCATION** as the variable. *Press* **D** (for Distribution).

	FREQUENCY	%
NO COLLEGE	11	2.5
SOME COLL.	18	4.1
COLL GRAD.	126	29.0
GRAD SCHOL	280	64.4

Nearly all members of the House are college graduates, and about two-thirds of them have gone beyond the bachelor's degree.

Use **5** or **RACE/ETHNI** as the variable. *Press* **D** (for Distribution).

	FREQUENCY	%
WHITE	376	86.4
AFRICAN-AM	38	8.7
HISPANIC	17	3.9
ASIAN	4	0.9

Non-Hispanic whites are overrepresented in the House. In 1990, 12.3 percent of Americans were African American, 2.7 percent were Asian, 8.2 percent were Hispanic, and 0.7 percent were Native American. African Americans come closest to being represented in proportion to their percentage of the population. The racial and ethnic make-up of the House is exactly the same in the 104th as in the 103rd Congress.

Use **7** or **RELIGION** as the variable. *Press* **D** (for Distribution).

	FREQUENCY	%
CATHOLIC	128	29.4
LIB. PROT.	160	36.8
CON. PROT.	80	18.4
JEW	25	5.7
OTHER	42	9.7

Catholics are represented in the House in proportion to their share of the population. Liberal Protestants are extremely overrepresented in the House, and Jews make up only about 2 percent of the population but are nearly 6 percent of House members. In contrast, conservative

Exercise 11: Who's in the House and Senate?

Protestants are extremely underrepresented—they make up about 30 percent of the general public. That is, the House has an oversupply of Episcopalians, Presbyterians, Methodists, Lutherans, Unitarians and other liberal denominations, and an undersupply of Baptists, Nazarenes, Seventh-day Adventists, Assemblies of God, various Pentecostals, and other conservative groups. However, the number of conservative Protestants increased from 67 to 80 in the 104th Congress.

Use **15** or **LAWYER?** as the variable. *Press* **D** (for Distribution).

	FREQUENCY	%
LAWYER	180	41.4
NON-LAWYER	255	58.6

Although a substantial minority of representatives are lawyers, the number declined by 10 in the 104th Congress.

Use **17** or **# TERMS** as the variable. *Press* **D** (for Distribution).

	FREQUENCY	%
ONE	86	19.8
2–4	170	39.1
5–8	102	23.4
9 OR MORE	77	17.7

There are 86 new members in the 104th Congress, while 77 members have served 9 or more terms.

Now let's examine the new members of the House. Return to the main menu and select **Tabular Statistics**. Use **9** or **PARTY** as the row variable and **16** or **NEWCOMERS** as the column variable. *Press* <ENTER> *twice* to skip the control variable and subset option. *Press* **C** for column percentages and the following table will appear.

	HOLDOVER	NEW REP
DEMOCRAT	54.9	15.1
REPUBLICAN	45.1	84.9

The new members of the House overwhelmingly are Republicans (84.9%), reflecting the surprise national landslide that gave Republicans control of Congress for the first time since 1954.

WORKSHEET

NAME:

COURSE:

DATE:

EXERCISE 11

Workbook exercises and software are copyrighted. Copying is prohibited by law.

1. Open the **SENATE** data set and select the **Univariate Statistics** function. Use **3** or **REGION** as the variable. When the pie chart appears, *press* **D** (for Distribution) and fill in the distribution below.

	FREQUENCY	%
EAST		
MIDWEST		
SOUTH		
WEST		

Which region has the most senators? _____

Which region has the least? _____

Compared with representatives, is this similar or different? (circle one)   SIMILAR   DIFFERENT

2. Use **4** or **PARTY** as the variable. *Press* **D** (for Distribution) and fill in the distribution below.

	FREQUENCY	%
DEMOCRAT		
REPUBLICAN		

Which party has the majority of senators? _____

Is this similar to or quite different from the party make-up of the House? (circle one)   SIMILAR   DIFFERENT

Exercise 11: Who's in the House and Senate?

WORKSHEET	EXERCISE 11

3. Use **7** or **RACE/ETH** as the variable. *Press D* (for Distribution) and fill in the distribution below.

	FREQUENCY	%
WHITE		
BLACK		
ASIAN		
NAT.AMER.		

How many African Americans are in the Senate? _____

Is this a larger or smaller percentage than in the House? (circle one)   LARGER   SMALLER

How many Asians are in the Senate? _____

Is this a larger or smaller percentage than in the House? (circle one)   LARGER   SMALLER

Based on these comparisons, are minorities (non-whites) better represented in the House or in the Senate? (circle one)   HOUSE   SENATE

4. Use **6** or **SEX** as the variable. *Press D* (for Distribution) and fill in the distribution below.

	FREQUENCY	%
MALE		
FEMALE		

What percentage of senators are female? _____

Is this very different from or similar to the gender make-up of the House? (circle one)   SIMILAR   DIFFERENT

5. Use **8** or **AGE** as the variable. *Press D* (for Distribution) and fill in the distribution below.

	FREQUENCY	%
OVER 60		
50–60		
UNDER 50		

NAME _____   **EXERCISE 11**

    What percentage of senators are under age 50? _____

    What percentage of members of the House are under age 45? _____

    What percentage of senators are over age 60? _____

    What percentage of members of the House are over age 65? _____

6. Use **12** or **LAWYER?** as the variable. *Press* **D** *(for Distribution) and fill in the distribution below.*

	FREQUENCY	%
LAWYER		
NOT		

    What percentage of senators are lawyers? _____

    Is this very different from or similar to the percentage of lawyers in the House? (circle one)   SIMILAR   DIFFERENT

7. Use **9** or **RELIGION** as the variable. *Press* **D** *(for Distribution) and fill in the distribution below.*

	FREQUENCY	%
CATHOLIC		
LIB.PROT.		
CON.PROT.		
JEW		
OTHER		

    Which religious group has the largest percentage of senators? _____

    Is this a larger or smaller percentage than in the House? (circle one)   LARGER   SMALLER

    How many conservative Protestants are in the Senate? _____

    Is this a larger or smaller percentage than in the House? (circle one)   LARGER   SMALLER

    How many Jews are in the Senate? _____

Exercise 11: Who's in the House and Senate?

WORKSHEET

EXERCISE 11

Is this a larger or smaller percentage than in the House? (circle one) LARGER   SMALLER

8. Go to the **Tabular Statistics** function and use **4** or **PARTY** as the row variable and **13** or **NEWCOMER?** as the column variable. When the table appears, *press* **C** for column percentages and fill in the table below.

	HOLDOVER	NEWCOMER
DEMOCRAT	%	%
REPUBLICAN	%	%

How many new members of the Senate are Democrats? _____

Is this a larger or smaller percentage than in the House? (circle one) LARGER   SMALLER

9. Based on these data, complete the portrait of the typical member of each house as begun below.

TYPICAL REPRESENTATIVE
Male
Republican

TYPICAL SENATOR
Male
Republican

◆ EXERCISE 12 ◆

Congressional Parties and the Contract with America

In this exercise you will contrast the make-up of congressional political parties and see how the parties differ ideologically as you trace the votes on the Republican Contract with America during the first 100 days of the 104th Congress.

One of the most important factors governing who is in Congress and how they vote is *who sent them?* This is especially true for members of the House since their districts are relatively small and often quite homogeneous in terms of economic, cultural, racial, and ethnic make-up. So, we will start by seeing how various aspects of congressional districts determine who they elect to the House.

Open the **HOUSE** data file and go to the **Tabular Statistics** function. Use **9** or **PARTY** as the row variable and use **20** or **FAM.INCOME** as the column variable. *Press <ENTER> twice* to skip the control variable and subset options. When the table appears, *press* **C** for column percentages. The following table will appear:

	OVER $40K	$30–$40K	$25–$30K	UNDER $25K
DEMOCRAT	30.1	40.2	46.3	71.0
REPUBLICAN	69.9	59.8	53.7	29.0

This measure of **family income** is not the family income of representatives—their congressional salaries are $129,500 a year. It is the annual median family income of their districts. What this table shows is that wealthy districts tend to elect Republicans (69.9 percent of representatives from districts having a median family income of $40,000 or more are Republicans), while poor districts tend to vote for Democrats—about 70 percent of House members from districts with an income below $25,000 are Democrats.

Use **9** or **PARTY** as the row variable and use **18** or **% AFRI-AM.** as the column variable. *Press* **C** for column percentages. The following table will appear:

	50% OR +	15%–49%	6%–14%	0%–5%
DEMOCRAT	100.0	67.1	44.4	35.9
REPUBLICAN	0.0	32.9	55.6	64.1

Here we see that when African Americans make up 50 percent or more of the voting-age population of a congressional district, the representative of that district is a Democrat. Only when a district contains less than 15 percent African Americans is its representative more apt to be a Republican than a Democrat. This is entirely consistent with what we found in Exercises 5 and 7—African-American voters overwhelmingly vote for Democrats.

Use **9** or **PARTY** as the row variable and use **19** or **%HISPANIC** as the column variable. *Press* **C** for column percentages. The following table will appear:

	50% OR +	10%–49%	3%–9%	UNDER 3%
DEMOCRAT	82.4	54.5	43.4	43.1
REPUBLICAN	17.6	45.5	56.6	56.9

Districts where half or more of the voting-age population is Hispanic also are very likely to elect Democrats, but not always.

Use **9** or **PARTY** as the row variable and use **6** or **WH/AF/HI** as the column variable. Do **NOT** percentage the table, but examine the raw frequencies instead.

	WHITE	AFRICAN-AM	HISPANIC
DEMOCRAT	151	36	14
REPUBLICAN	224	2	3

Notice that of the 38 African-American members of the House, there are only 2 Republicans, while of 17 Hispanic members there are 3 Republicans.

Use **9** or **PARTY** as the row variable and use **12** or **SEX** as the column variable. *Press C* for column percentages. The following table will appear:

	MALE	FEMALE
DEMOCRAT	45.0	63.8
REPUBLICAN	55.0	36.2

Women in the House also are apt to be Democrats.

Use **9** or **PARTY** as the row variable and use **15** or **LAWYER?** as the column variable. *Press C* for column percentages. The following table will appear:

	LAWYER	NON-LAWYER
DEMOCRAT	53.3	42.5
REPUBLICAN	46.7	57.5

Lawyers are more likely to be Democrats.

Use **9** or **PARTY** as the row variable and use **8** or **RELIGION 3** as the column variable. *Press C* for column percentages. The following table will appear:

	CATHOLIC	PROTESTANT	JEWISH
DEMOCRAT	55.5	40.8	83.3
REPUBLICAN	44.5	59.2	16.7

Jews are the religious group most apt to be Democrats and Protestants are the least apt. But these figures obscure something interesting. To see what it is use **8** or **RELIGION 3** as the row variable and use **6** or **WH/AF/HI** as the column variable. *Press C* for column percentages. The following table will appear:

	WHITE	AFRICAN-AM	HISPANIC
CATHOLIC	32.6	8.8	87.5
PROTESTANT	60.0	91.2	12.5
JEWISH	7.4	0.0	0.0

African Americans are overwhelmingly Protestants (three are Catholics), and all but two African Americans in the House are Democrats. This elevates the percentage of Protestants who are Democrats. To a lesser degree, Hispanic Americans elevate the percentage of Democrats among Catholics. To observe these effects let's recreate the table limiting it to white representatives.

Use **9** or **PARTY** as the row variable, use **8** or **RELIGION 3** as the column variable, and use **6** or **WH/AF/HI** as the subset variable making **1** both the lower and the upper limit. *Press* **C** for column percentages. The following table will appear:

	CATHOLIC	PROTESTANT	JEWISH
DEMOCRAT	50.5	32.4	83.3
REPUBLICAN	49.5	67.6	16.7

Now we see that among whites most Protestants are Republicans.

The Republican Contract with America played a major role in giving them control of both houses. There were 10 major provisions in the contract and, in addition, Republicans promised that on the first day of the new Congress they would pass a number of reforms in the way Congress functions. Among these was the promise to ban the casting of proxy votes in committee—that, rather than send members of their staffs to vote for them, members would have to be present in order to vote.

Use **22** or **NO PROXIES** as the row variable and use **9** or **PARTY** as the column variable. *Press* **C** for column percentages. The following table will appear:

	DEMOCRAT	REPUBLICAN
NO	6.4	0.0
YES	93.6	100.0

The new rule breezed through—only 13 Democrats voted no and all Republicans voted yes. A second promise for the first day was to limit the terms of all committee chairs to eight years.

Use **21** or **LEAD.LIMIT** as the row variable and use **9** or **PARTY** as the column variable. *Press* **C** for column percentages. The following table will appear:

	DEMOCRAT	REPUBLICAN
NO	36.5	0.0
YES	63.5	100.0

The Democrats were not quite as cooperative when this bill passed, but once again all of the Republicans voted yes.

Perhaps the most significant first-day legislation promised by the Republicans in their Contract was to require a three-fifths majority vote (rather than only a simple majority) to pass any tax increases.

Use **23** or **TAX UP 3/5** as the row variable and use **9** or **PARTY** as the column variable. *Press* **C** for column percentages. The following table will appear:

	DEMOCRAT	REPUBLICAN
NO	74.4	0.0
YES	25.6	100.0

On this proposal the Democrats balked and three-fourths of them voted no. Once again all Republicans voted yes.

To understand this result better, use **3** or **REGION** as the row variable and use **23** or **TAX UP 3/5** as the column variable. Then use **9** or **PARTY** as the subset variable, making **1** both the lower and the upper limit. This limits the table to Democrats. When the table appears, *press* **C** for column percentages. This table will be on the screen:

TAX UP 3/5

	NO	YES
EAST	27.2	11.5
MIDWEST	22.5	21.2
SOUTH	27.8	55.8
WEST	22.5	11.5

Here we can see that 55.8 percent of those Democrats who did not stay with the party and who voted with the Republicans on this bill were *Southern* Democrats.

There is another way to see this. Use **23** or **TAX UP 3/5** as the row variable and use **10** or **SOUTH DEM** as the column variable. *Press* **C** for column percentages. The following table will appear:

	DEMOCRAT	S.DEMOCRAT	REPUBLICAN
NO	82.6	59.2	0.0
YES	17.4	40.8	100.0

Here we see that non-Southern Democrats overwhelmingly opposed the 3/5th tax bill while nearly 41 percent of Southern Democrats voted yes. As a group, Southern Democrats are more moderate than either non-Southern Democrats or Republicans.

Use **36** or **REG.MORAT** as the row variable and use **10** or **SOUTH DEM** as the column variable. *Press* **C** for column percentages. The following table will appear:

	DEMOCRAT	S.DEMOCRAT	REPUBLICAN
NO	84.4	53.0	0.9
YES	15.6	47.0	99.1

This bill also was part of the Contract, and imposed a temporary moratorium that prohibited federal agencies from implementing any new federal regulations. While the Republicans did not need the votes of Southern Democrats to pass the bill, they received nearly half of them.

Use **27** or **DEATH PEN1** as the row variable and use **10** or **SOUTH DEM** as the column variable. *Press* **C** for column percentages. The following table will appear:

	DEMOCRAT	S.DEMOCRAT	REPUBLICAN
NO	74.6	46.5	0.4
YES	25.4	53.5	99.6

Another part of the Contract involved limiting the ability of prisoners to delay the death penalty by exploiting the courts. This bill limits prisoners to one habeas corpus petition and requires that such petitions be filed within two years for federal cases and one year for state cases. The majority of Southern Democrats joined the Republicans in passing the bill, while three-fourths of non-Southern Democrats voted no.

WORKSHEET

NAME:

COURSE:

DATE:

EXERCISE 12

Workbook exercises and software are copyrighted. Copying is prohibited by law.

1. Using the **HOUSE** data set and the **Tabular Statistics** function, create and fill in the following table: row variable: **9** or **PARTY**; column variable: **18** or **% AFRI-AM**. Use **5** or **RACE/ETHNI** as the subset variable, and use **2** as both the low and the high value of the subset. Thus the table will be limited to **African-American** representatives. **Do NOT percentage the table. Fill in the raw numbers below.**

	50% OR +	15%–49%	6%–14%	0%–5%
DEMOCRAT				
REPUBLICAN				

Keeping in mind that these are only the African-American representatives, how do the Democrats differ from the two Republicans in terms of the racial composition of their districts?

Given what you know about voting patterns, explain why it might be very hard for an African-American Republican to be elected to Congress.

2. Using the **SENATE** data set and **Tabular Statistics**, create and fill in the following table. Row variable: **4** or **PARTY**; column variable: **6** or **SEX**. (Remember to percentage the columns.)

	MALE	FEMALE
DEMOCRAT	%	%
REPUBLICAN	%	%

To which party do most women belong? _____

Is this result similar to or different from that of the House? (circle one)   SIMILAR   DIFFERENT

Exercise 12: Congressional Parties and the Contract With America

WORKSHEET	EXERCISE 12

3. Create and fill in the table below. Row variable: **4** or **PARTY**; column variable: **12** or **LAWYER**.

	LAWYER	NOT
DEMOCRAT	%	%
REPUBLICAN	%	%

    To which party do most lawyers belong? _____

    Is the difference statistically significant? (circle one)   YES   NO

    Prob. = _____

4. Create and fill in the table below. Row variable: **4** or **PARTY**; column variable: **20** or **RELIGION 3**.

	CATHOLIC	PROTESTANT	JEW
DEMOCRAT	%	%	%
REPUBLICAN	%	%	%

    To which party do most Catholics belong? _____

    To which party do most Protestants belong? _____

    To which party do most Jews belong? _____

    Is the difference statistically significant? (circle one)   YES   NO

    Prob. = _____

    Is this result similar to or different from that of the House? (circle one)   SIMILAR   DIFFERENT

5. Create and fill in the table below. Row variable: **4** or **PARTY**; column variable: **8** or **AGE**.

	OVER 60	50–60	UNDER 50
DEMOCRAT	%	%	%
REPUBLICAN	%	%	%

NAME _____ EXERCISE 12

To which party do most over 60 belong? _____

To which party do most 50–60 belong? _____

To which party do most under 50 belong? _____

Is the difference statistically significant? (circle one) YES   NO

Prob. = _____

6. Create and fill in the table below. Row variable: **18** or **BAL.BUDG.**; column variable: **5** or **SOUTH DEM**.

	DEMOCRAT	SOUTH DEMO	REPUBLICAN
NO	%	%	%
YES	%	%	%

Are these differences statistically significant? (circle one) YES   NO

Prob. = _____

What is the value of Cramer's V? V = _____

7. Create and fill in the table below. Row variable: **19** or **LINE VETO**; column variable: **5** or **SOUTH DEM**.

	DEMOCRAT	SOUTH DEMO	REPUBLICAN
NO	%	%	%
YES	%	%	%

Are these differences statistically significant? (circle one) YES   NO

Prob. = _____

What is the value of Cramer's V? V = _____

Exercise 12: Congressional Parties and the Contract With America

| WORKSHEET | | | EXERCISE 12 |

8. Switching to the **HOUSE** data set, create and fill in the table below. Row variable: **26** or **LINE VETO**; column variable: **10** or **SOUTH DEM**.

	DEMOCRAT	SOUTH DEMO	REPUBLICAN
NO	%	%	%
YES	%	%	%

Are these differences statistically significant? (circle one)   YES   NO

Prob. = _____

Is this result rather similar to or different from
that of the Senate? (circle one)   SIMILAR   DIFFERENT

9. Taking all of these findings into account, discuss the claim that there are three, not two, parties in Congress.

◆ EXERCISE 13 ◆
Congressional Campaign Finances

A primary fact of life facing every elected official is that the next election is always just around the corner and it costs money to win elections. Since they are up for re-election every two years, many members of the House are never really able to cease campaigning. And, while senators face re-election only every six years, their campaigns usually cost a lot more since theirs is a statewide office. Thus, perhaps the single most central aspect of campaigning is fund-raising. In this exercise we will see how much money members of Congress raise and where they get their campaign funds.

Open the **HOUSE** data file and go to the **Univariate Statistics** function. Use **43** or **CAMPAIGN $** as the variable. When the screen asks for a subset variable, simply *press* <ENTER> to continue. *Press* **D** (for Distribution) to see this distribution.

	FREQUENCY	%
OVER $500K	215	49.4
UNDER $500	220	50.6

Approximately half of the representatives raised more than $500,000 for their 1992 campaign. Congressman Richard A. Gephardt (Democrat from Missouri) raised the most: $2,485,000. Next was Robert K. Dornan (Republican of California) with $2,296,000. At the other end of the spectrum, William F. Goodling (Republican of Pennsylvania) raised a grand total of $51,000 and Andrew Jacobs (Democrat of Indiana) raised $12,000.

Switch to the **SENATE** data set and go to the **Univariate Statistics** function. Use **23** or **CAMPAIGN $** as the variable. After the bar graph is on the screen, *press* **D** (for Distribution) to see this distribution:

	FREQUENCY	%
OVER $3 M	56	56.0
UNDER $3 M	44	44.0

In general, it costs a lot more to run for the Senate than for the House; hence more than half of senators raised more than $3 million to finance their most recent election. At the top was Jesse Helms, Republican of North Carolina, who raised $17,751,029. Nancy Landon Kassebaum, Republican of Kansas, raised the least: $520,471.

Other things being equal it costs more to run for the Senate in a large state than in a small one— TV time is much cheaper in small markets, for one thing. So, a more equitable way to look at campaign spending is in terms of costs per vote. That is, how much was spent for each vote received? Use **22** or **$ PER VOTE** as the variable.

	FREQUENCY	%
OVER $6	41	41.8
UNDER $6	57	58.2

Exercise 13: Congressional Campaign Finances

Over 40 percent of senators spent more than $6 in campaign funds for each vote they received. At the top was Joseph Biden (Democrat of Delaware), who spent $22.58. Again, it was Nancy Landon Kassebaum who spent the least: 90 cents.

Switch to the **HOUSE** data set and select the univariate task again. Use **42** or **$ PER VOTE** as the variable.

	FREQUENCY	%
OVER $7	113	28.5
$4–7	151	38.1
UNDER $4	132	33.3

There is far more variation among representatives than among senators in the amount they spend per vote—hence the use of three spending categories. More than 100 representatives spent more than $7 per vote. Republican Robert Dornan (Calif.) spent the most—$49.12—while Andrew Jacobs (Dem., Ind.) spent 22 cents.

Now let's see where all of this money comes from. Switch back to the **SENATE** data set. Use **21** or **% PAC $** as the variable.

	FREQUENCY	%
UNDER 20%	21	21.2
20–40%	54	54.5
OVER 40%	24	24.2

Here we see that the majority of senators received a substantial part of their funding from Political Action Committees, or PACs. Almost any organization—a corporation, a union, a professional association, a neighborhood club, or even a bowling team—can create its own political action committee and then raise funds from member contributions or even by seeking outside donations. While no individual may contribute more than $1,000 per year to any political candidate, a PAC can contribute $5,000. Moreover, PACs can easily be multiplied so that the same interest group can sustain many PACs, each permitted to contribute $5,000 to an individual candidate.

The two Democrats from North Dakota, Kent Conrad (77%) and Byron Dorgan (75%), received the highest proportion of their total campaign funds from PACs. In contrast, two other Democrats, Herbert Kohl of Wisconsin and Edward Kennedy of Massachusetts, received no PAC funds at all (although both had done so in previous elections).

Switch to the **HOUSE** data set. Use **41** or **% PAC $** as the variable.

	FREQUENCY	%
OVER 60%	96	22.1
41–60%	144	33.2
20–40%	126	29.0
UNDER 20%	68	15.7

Here too there is more variation in the House than in the Senate. Floyd Spence (Rep. S.C.) and Cardiss Collins (Dem., Ill.) each got 81 percent of their funds from PACs. In contrast, 18 representatives received no PAC funds.

WORKSHEET

NAME:

COURSE:

DATE:

EXERCISE

13

Workbook exercises and software are copyrighted. Copying is prohibited by law.

1. Using the **HOUSE** data set and **Tabular Statistics**, create and fill in the following table. Row variable: **41** or **% PAC $**; column variable: **9** or **PARTY**. (Remember to percentage the columns in all of the tables for this exercise.)

	DEMOCRAT	REPUBLICAN
OVER 60%	%	%
41–60%	%	%
20–40%	%	%
UNDER 20%	%	%

Are Democrats or Republicans more likely to receive 60 percent or more of their funds from PACs? _____

Are these differences significant? (circle one)   YES   NO

Prob. = _____

What is the value of Cramer's V?   V = _____

Did this result surprise you? Explain.

2. Create and fill in the following table. Row variable: **41** or **% PAC $**; column variable: **12** or **SEX**.

	MALE	FEMALE
OVER 60%	%	%
41–60%	%	%
20–40%	%	%
UNDER 20%	%	%

Exercise 13: Congressional Campaign Finances

WORKSHEET	EXERCISE 13

Are males or females more likely to receive 60 percent or more of their funds from PACs? _____

Are these differences significant? (circle one)   YES   NO

Prob. = _____

What is the value of Cramer's V?   V = _____

Did this result surprise you? Explain.

3. Create and fill in the following table. Row variable: **41** or **% PAC $**; column variable: **40** or **LEADER 103**. (Note: This refers to leaders in the 103rd Congress since the money was raised prior to the 1994 election, during the time when congressional leadership rested entirely in the hands of the Democrats.)

	LEADER	NOT LEADER
OVER 60%	%	%
41–60%	%	%
20–40%	%	%
UNDER 20%	%	%

Write in the long label of **40** or **LEADER 103**.

_____

Are leaders in the House more or less likely than ordinary members to receive 60 percent or more of their funds from PACs? _____

Are these differences significant? (circle one)   YES   NO

Prob. = _____

What is the value of Cramer's V?   V = _____

NAME _____ EXERCISE 13

4. Create and fill in the following table. Row variable: **41** or **% PAC $**; column variable: **17** or **# TERMS**. (Remember, you should be using column percentaging for your tables.)

	ONE	2 TO 4	5 TO 8	9 OR MORE
OVER 60%	%	%	%	%
41–60%	%	%	%	%
20–40%	%	%	%	%
UNDER 20%	%	%	%	%

Write in the long label of **17** or **# TERMS**.

_____

Are members of the House who have served 9 or more terms more or less likely than first-term members to receive 60 percent or more of their funds from PACs? _____

Are these differences significant? (circle one)   YES   NO

Prob. = _____

What is the value of Cramer's V?   V = _____

Discuss why PACs are more likely to give money to leaders and members with the most seniority.

5. Create and fill in the following table. Row variable: **41** or **% PAC $**; column variable: **16** or **NEWCOMERS**.

	HOLDOVER	NEW REP
OVER 60%	%	%
41–60%	%	%
20–40%	%	%
UNDER 20%	%	%

Exercise 13: Congressional Campaign Finances

WORKSHEET	EXERCISE 13

Are holdover or new members more likely to receive 60 percent or more of their funds from PACs? _____

Are these differences significant? (circle one)   YES   NO

Prob. = _____

What is the value of Cramer's V?   V = _____

6. Looking at all of the preceding results, discuss the probability that the new Republican Congress will put new limits on PACs. There is no "right" answer—simply explain why you think they will or won't.

♦ OPTIONAL CHALLENGE ASSIGNMENT ♦

Prompted by the findings in this exercise, explore the data set for the **OLDHOUSE** and **OLDSEN** to see if the same patterns existed in the 103rd Congress.

◆ EXERCISE 14 ◆
A Female or African-American President

Back in 1937, the Gallup Poll first asked a national sample of Americans if they would be willing to vote for a woman for president of the United States. Only a third said that they would. When the question was repeated in 1955, slightly more than half (52%) said they would be willing to vote for a woman. By 1977 support for a woman reached 77 percent. Let's see where things stand today.

Open the **NORC93** data set and select the **Univariate Statistics** function. Use **39** or **WOMAN PREZ** as the variable. *Press* **D** (for Distribution) and this distribution will appear below this question:

If your party nominated a woman for President, would you vote for her if she were qualified for the job?

	FREQUENCY	%
YES	936	90.7
NO	96	9.3

The proportion of Americans willing to vote for a woman for president had reached almost 91 percent by 1993. Still, 1 person out of 10 would not vote to put a woman in the White House. In this exercise we will see what sort of person would not support a woman for president.

In 1958, as the Civil Rights Movement gathered momentum, the Gallup Poll asked a national sample of Americans if they would be willing to vote for a black for president. Only 38 percent said yes. By 1971, 70 percent answered yes. Let's see how things stand now.

Use **44** or **BLACK PREZ** as the variable.

If your party nominated a black for President, would you vote for him if he were qualified for the job?

	FREQUENCY	%
YES	909	88.9
NO	113	11.1

Nearly the same percentage is obtained here as those who say they would vote for a woman for president.

In this exercise we also will see what kinds of people will and will not vote for an African American for president.

Switch to the **Tabular Statistics** function and use **39** or **WOMAN PREZ** as the row variable and **85** or **DEM/REP** as the column variable. *Press* **C** for column percentages. This table will appear:

	DEMOCRAT	REPUBLICAN
YES	92.3	88.7
NO	7.7	11.3

It looks as if Democrats are slightly more likely to vote for a woman for president. *Press* **S** (for Statistics). But the difference is not significant.

Use **39** or **WOMAN PREZ** as the row variable and use **23** or **REGION** as the column variable. *Press* **C** for column percentages. The following table will appear:

	EAST	MIDWEST	SOUTH	WEST
YES	92.2	83.6	89.2	91.4
NO	7.8	16.4	10.8	8.6

Nor does region matter. By this point even a very experienced survey analyst might be somewhat frustrated. "Everybody" knows that Republicans and Southerners tend to be far less liberated from traditional beliefs about proper gender roles. The trouble is that what everybody knows frequently is wrong—as it is in this instance. If it were easy to know how various groups stand on issues, no one would spend hundreds of thousands of dollars for a national survey to find out.

Use **39** or **WOMAN PREZ** as the row variable and use **8** or **RACE** as the column variable. *Press* **C** for column percentages. The following table will appear:

	WHITE	AFRICAN-AM
YES	90.1	94.4
NO	9.9	5.6

Here we can see that race doesn't matter.

So, let's try something that is certain to work. Surely, conservative Protestants will be less willing than liberal Protestants and Catholics to support a woman for president.

Use **39** or **WOMAN PREZ** as the row variable and use **86** or **CATH/PROT** as the column variable. *Press* **C** for column percentages. The following table will appear:

	CATHOLIC	LIB.PROT	CONS.PROT
YES	92.1	90.8	87.2
NO	7.9	9.2	12.8

Once again the obvious isn't so. These differences are not statistically significant.

Use **39** or **WOMAN PREZ** as the row variable and use **13** or **CH. ATTEND** as the column variable. *Press* **C** for column percentages. The following table will appear:

	WEEKLY	MONTHLY	YEARLY	SELDOM/NEV
YES	86.2	93.2	94.7	93.3
NO	13.8	6.8	5.3	6.7

Finally. Church attendance does produce a slightly negative effect on willingness to vote for a woman. Although the result is statistically significant, it is rather small and limited: Weekly attenders are modestly less willing to vote for a woman, but other variations in attendance result in no significant differences.

To see this for yourself, use **39** or **WOMAN PREZ** as the row variable and use **13** or **CH. ATTEND** as the column variable. Then use **13** or **CH. ATTEND** again as the subset variable, limiting the data to a low value of 2 and a high value of 4. *Press* **C** for column percentages. The following table will appear:

	WEEKLY	MONTHLY	YEARLY	SELDOM/NEV
YES	0	93.2	94.7	93.3
NO	0	6.8	5.3	6.7

Press **S** (for Statistics). Now, with the weekly attenders omitted from the table, the differences are not significant.

But, surely this will produce differences. Use **39** or **WOMAN PREZ** as the row variable and use **32** or **CAR RACES?** as the column variable. *Press* **C** for column percentages. The following table will appear:

	ATTENDED	DID NOT
YES	89.8	90.8
NO	10.2	9.2

Amazing. People who have attended an "auto, stock car, or motorcycle race" in the past year are not less willing to vote for a woman.

But enough of this. Here's the one you have been waiting for.

Use **39** or **WOMAN PREZ** as the row variable and use **6** or **SEX** as the column variable. *Press* **C** for column percentages. The following table will appear:

	MALE	FEMALE
YES	90.2	91.1
NO	9.8	8.9

No! Men are not more likely than women to reject a woman for president.

Use **39** or **WOMAN PREZ** as the row variable and use **7** or **AGE** as the column variable. *Press* **C** for column percentages. The following table will appear:

	18–29	30–39	40–49	50–65	OVER 65
YES	95.1	95.1	93.8	89.1	78.6
NO	4.9	4.9	6.2	10.9	21.4

There is an age effect, but only at the upper end. That is, people over 65 are somewhat less likely to be willing to vote for a woman for president, but among younger people age differences are negligible.

Finally, use **39** or **WOMAN PREZ** as the row variable and use **17** or **EDUCATION** as the column variable. *Press* **C** for column percentages. The following table will appear:

Exercise 14: A Female or African-American President

	NOT HS GRAD	HS GRAD	SOME COLL.	COLL GRAD
YES	83.9	90.6	91.6	95.3
NO	16.1	9.4	8.4	4.7

There is a modest, but significant, education effect: People who did not finish high school are a bit less willing to support a woman. This probably is really an age effect, since people who didn't finish high school tend also to be older.

So, that's how to find out who would vote for a woman. Now, it's your turn to find out who would or would not vote for an African-American candidate for president.

WORKSHEET

NAME:

COURSE:

DATE:

EXERCISE 14

Workbook exercises and software are copyrighted. Copying is prohibited by law.

1. Using the **NORC93** data set and Tabular Statistics, create and fill in the following table. Row variable: **44** or **BLACK PREZ**; column variable: **8** or **RACE**. (Remember to do column percentaging.)

	WHITE	AFRICAN-AM
YES	%	%
NO	%	%

Is the difference significant? (circle one)   YES   NO

Prob. = _____

What is the value of Cramer's V?   V = _____

2. Create and fill in the following table. Row variable: **44** or **BLACK PREZ**; column variable: **85** or **DEM/REP**.

	DEMOCRAT	REPUBLICAN
YES	%	%
NO	%	%

Are Democrats or Republicans more likely to support an African American for president? _____

Is the difference significant? (circle one)   YES   NO

Prob. = _____

What is the value of Cramer's V?   V = _____

Exercise 14: A Female or African-American President

| WORKSHEET | | | EXERCISE 14 |

3. Create and fill in the following table. Row variable: **44** or **BLACK PREZ**; column variable: **5** or **LIB./CONS.**.

	LIBERAL	MODERATE	CONSERV.
YES	%	%	%
NO	%	%	%

Are liberals, moderates, or conservatives more likely to support an African American for president? _____

Are these differences significant? (circle one)   YES   NO

Prob. = _____

What is the value of Cramer's V?   V = _____

4. Create and fill in the following table. Row variable: **44** or **BLACK PREZ**; column variable: **15** or **VETERAN?**.

	VETERAN	NON-VET
YES	%	%
NO	%	%

Are these differences significant? (circle one)   YES   NO

Prob. = _____

What is the value of Cramer's V?   V = _____

5. Create and fill in the following table. Row variable: **44** or **BLACK PREZ**; column variable: **31** or **TV PBS**.

	DAILY	WEEKLY	MONTHLY	RARELY
YES	%	%	%	%
NO	%	%	%	%

*Write in the long label for **31 TV PBS**.*

_____

Are these differences significant? (circle one)   YES   NO

NAME	EXERCISE 14

Prob. = _____

What is the value of Cramer's V?   V = _____

6. Many political commentators assume that veterans are conservative and that people who frequently watch public television are liberals. Assuming this to be true, looking back over these results, discuss the claim that African Americans overwhelmingly support Democrats and liberals *because* Republicans and conservatives discriminate against African-American candidates.

7. Create and fill in the following table. Row variable: **44** or **BLACK PREZ**; column variable: **23** or **REGION**.

	EAST	MIDWEST	SOUTH	WEST
YES	%	%	%	%
NO	%	%	%	%

In which region are people more likely to support an African American for president? _____

In which region are people least likely to support an African American for president? _____

Are these differences significant? (circle one)   YES   NO

Prob. = _____

What is the value of Cramer's V?   V = _____

8. Create and fill in the following table. Row variable: **44** or **BLACK PREZ**; column variable: **7** or **AGE**.

	18–29	30–39	40–49	50–65	OVER 65
YES	%	%	%	%	%
NO	%	%	%	%	%

Exercise 14: A Female or African-American President

WORKSHEET	EXERCISE 14

In which age group are people least likely to support an African American for president? _____

Are these differences significant? (circle one)   YES   NO

Prob. = _____

What is the value of Cramer's V?   V = _____

9. Create and fill in the following table. Row variable: **44** or **BLACK PREZ**; column variable: **17** or **EDUCATION**.

	NOT HS GRAD	HS GRAD	SOME COLL.	COLL GRAD
YES	%	%	%	%
NO	%	%	%	%

In which education group are people more likely to support an African American for president? _____

In which education group are people least likely to support an African American for president? _____

Are these differences significant? (circle one)   YES   NO

Prob. = _____

What is the value of Cramer's V?   V = _____

10. Considering the results for age and education, what might we expect about willingness to vote for an African-American candidate in the future?

♦ OPTIONAL CHALLENGE ASSIGNMENT ♦

In the **NORC93** data set, 21 percent of Americans agreed: "Most men are better suited emotionally for politics than are most women." (See variable **40** or **MEN BETTER**.) Drawing hints from the findings about voting for a woman for president, find out who thinks men are better suited for politics.

♦ EXERCISE 15 ♦
Confidence in Government

Effective government rests upon public confidence and, of course, public confidence tends to rest upon effective government. In recent years there has been a noticeable decrease both in public confidence in government and in the ability of government to meet public expectations.

So, in this exercise you will explore and compare levels of public confidence in the three branches of the federal government and contrast these levels of confidence with confidence in other major social institutions.

Open the **NORC93** data set and select the **Univariate Statistics** function. Use **59** or **CONGRESS?** as the variable.

I am going to name some institutions in this country. As far as the people running these institutions are concerned, would you say you have a great deal of confidence, or only some confidence, or hardly any confidence at all in them?

CONGRESS

	FREQUENCY	%
GREAT DEAL	73	7.1
ONLY SOME	528	51.3
HARDLY ANY	428	41.6

Americans have little confidence in Congress—only 7.1 percent express a great deal of confidence and 41.6 percent said they had "hardly any confidence" in Congress.

Use **54** or **EX.BRANCH** as the variable.

THE EXECUTIVE BRANCH

	FREQUENCY	%
GREAT DEAL	124	12.2
ONLY SOME	556	54.5
HARDLY ANY	340	33.3

The executive branch is slightly ahead of Congress in terms of public confidence, but the fact remains that few Americans have much confidence in it.

Use **58** or **SUP.COURT** as the variable.

THE SUPREME COURT

	FREQUENCY	%
GREAT DEAL	322	31.9
ONLY SOME	546	54.1
HARDLY ANY	141	14.0

Exercise 15: Confidence in Government

Almost a third of Americans express a great deal of confidence in the Supreme Court, and only 14 percent say they have hardly any confidence in the Court.

Altogether, Americans seem to have very little confidence in their government. Perhaps some comparisons with non-governmental institutions can help put these findings in perspective.

Use **55** or **LABOR?** as the variable.

ORGANIZED LABOR

	FREQUENCY	%
GREAT DEAL	87	8.9
ONLY SOME	553	56.4
HARDLY ANY	340	34.7

Americans have only slightly more confidence in labor unions than they do in Congress.

Use **56** or **PRESS?** as the variable.

THE PRESS

	FREQUENCY	%
GREAT DEAL	114	11.0
ONLY SOME	512	49.6
HARDLY ANY	406	39.3

The press does not earn high marks either, being about on a par with the executive branch.

Use **61** or **BIG BIZ?** as the variable.

MAJOR COMPANIES

	FREQUENCY	%
GREAT DEAL	221	21.8
ONLY SOME	661	65.3
HARDLY ANY	130	12.8

Americans have considerably more confidence in big business than in either Congress or the executive branch, but less confidence than they have in the Supreme Court.

Use **62** or **EDUCATIONC** as the variable.

EDUCATION

	FREQUENCY	%
GREAT DEAL	234	22.6
ONLY SOME	609	58.8
HARDLY ANY	192	18.6

Educational institutions inspire the same level of confidence as major companies.

Use **57** or **SCIENCE** as the variable.

THE SCIENTIFIC COMMUNITY

	FREQUENCY	%
GREAT DEAL	395	41.1
ONLY SOME	496	51.5
HARDLY ANY	71	7.4

The scientific community inspires a higher level of confidence than even the Supreme Court.

Use **60** or **MILITARY** as the variable.

THE MILITARY

	FREQUENCY	%
GREAT DEAL	441	42.6
ONLY SOME	477	46.1
HARDLY ANY	116	11.2

And the military earns the largest percentage who said they had a "great deal" of confidence. This undoubtedly was influenced by the performance of the armed forces during the Gulf War.

Open the **P1973–93** data set and select the **Tabular Statistics** function. Use **17** or **MILITARY** as the row variable and **1** or **YEAR** as the column variable. *Press* **C** for column percentages.

	1973	1993
GREAT DEAL	32.6	42.6
ONLY SOME	50.9	46.1
HARDLY ANY	16.5	11.2

As expected, confidence in the military has risen significantly.

Use **15** or **SCIENCE** as the row variable and **1** or **YEAR** as the column variable. *Press* **C** for column percentages.

	1973	1993
GREAT DEAL	40.8	41.1
ONLY SOME	52.0	51.6
HARDLY ANY	7.2	7.4

In contrast, confidence in science did not budge over the 20-year period.

In the remainder of this exercise you will focus on public confidence in Congress and in the military.

WORKSHEET

NAME:

COURSE:

DATE:

Workbook exercises and software are copyrighted. Copying is prohibited by law.

EXERCISE 15

1. Using the **NORC93** data set and **Tabular Statistics**, create and fill in the following table. Row variable: **59** or **CONGRESS?**; column variable: **6** or **SEX**. (Remember to do column percentaging for each table.)

	MALE	FEMALE
GREAT DEAL	%	%
ONLY SOME	%	%
HARDLY ANY	%	%

   Are males or females more likely to lack confidence in Congress? _____

   Is the difference significant? (circle one)   YES   NO

   Prob. = _____

2. Create and fill in the following table. Row variable: **59** or **CONGRESS?**; column variable: **85** or **DEM/REP**.

	DEMOCRAT	REPUBLICAN
GREAT DEAL	%	%
ONLY SOME	%	%
HARDLY ANY	%	%

   Are Democrats or Republicans more likely to lack confidence in Congress? _____

   Is the difference significant? (circle one)   YES   NO

   Prob. = _____

3. Create and fill in the following table. Row variable: **59** or **CONGRESS?**; column variable: **23** or **REGION**.

	EAST	MIDWEST	SOUTH	WEST
GREAT DEAL	%	%	%	%
ONLY SOME	%	%	%	%
HARDLY ANY	%	%	%	%

Exercise 15: Confidence in Government

WORKSHEET	EXERCISE 15

In which region are people more likely to lack confidence in Congress? _____

In which region are people more likely to have confidence in Congress? _____

Are these differences significant? (circle one) YES   NO

Prob. = _____

Look back to Exercise 1 and see if you can find a reason for these regional differences. Explain.

4. Create and fill in the following table. Row variable: **1** or **PRES IN 92**; column variable: **59** or **CONGRESS?**.

	GREAT DEAL	ONLY SOME	HARDLY ANY
CLINTON	%	%	%
BUSH	%	%	%
PEROT	%	%	%

Here people are divided into three groups on the basis of their expressed confidence in Congress.

In which group did Clinton run best? _____

In which group did Perot run best? _____

Are these differences significant? (circle one) YES   NO

Prob. = _____

In light of these results, discuss the idea that many people voted for Perot as a way of voting no.

NAME _____ EXERCISE 15

5. Create and fill in the following table. Row variable: **60** or **MILITARY?**; column variable: **6** or **SEX**.

	MALE	FEMALE
GREAT DEAL	%	%
ONLY SOME	%	%
HARDLY ANY	%	%

Are males or females more likely to have a great deal of confidence in the military? _____

Is the difference significant? (circle one)   YES   NO

Prob. = _____

6. Create and fill in the following table. Row variable: **60** or **MILITARY?**; column variable: **15** or **VETERAN?**.

	VETERAN	NON-VET
GREAT DEAL	%	%
ONLY SOME	%	%
HARDLY ANY	%	%

Are veterans or non-veterans more likely to have a great deal of confidence in the military? _____

Is the difference significant? (circle one)   YES   NO

Prob. = _____

Now recreate this table, using the subset function to limit the data to males. Use **6** or **SEX** as the subset variable and make **1** both the upper and lower limit.

	VETERAN	NON-VET
GREAT DEAL	%	%
ONLY SOME	%	%
HARDLY ANY	%	%

When only men are examined, are veterans or non-veterans more likely to have a great deal of confidence in the military? _____

Is the difference significant? (circle one)   YES   NO

Prob. = _____

Exercise 15: Confidence in Government

WORKSHEET	EXERCISE 15

7. Create and fill in the following table. Row variable: **1** or **PRES IN 92**; column variable: **60** or **MILITARY?**.

	GREAT DEAL	ONLY SOME	HARDLY ANY
CLINTON	%	%	%
BUSH	%	%	%
PEROT	%	%	%

Here people are divided into three groups on the basis of their expressed confidence in the military.

In which group did Clinton get the least support? _____

In which group did Bush run best? _____

Are these differences significant? (circle one)   YES   NO

Prob. = _____

Look back at Exercise 5 and identify a finding there that is similar to the finding above. Explain.

♦ OPTIONAL CHALLENGE ASSIGNMENT ♦

Use the **P1973–93** data set and explore changes in confidence in government, especially in Congress and the executive branch. Remember to always use **1** or **YEAR** as the column variable. To see if changes occurred in all age groups, all regions, among both whites and African Americans, or political parties, use these (one at a time) as control variables.

PART IV

FREEDOM

When people speak of America as a "free country," they have two basic kinds of freedom in mind. The first kind of freedom consists of what are called *civil liberties*. These include freedom of speech, press, religion, assembly, and petition. The Bill of Rights guarantees these freedoms from infringement by the government or by citizen-groups. If a mob shouts down a speaker, they are denying his or her civil liberties. If the government forbids an unpopular group from expressing their views, that too is a violation of their civil liberties.

The second kind of freedom consists of *civil rights*. These include all the rights of democratic citizenship including voting, equal treatment before the law, an equal share of public benefits, and equal access to public facilities. When blacks were excluded from voting and from jury duty, and denied access to parks and beaches in the South, they were being denied their civil rights.

In the next two exercises, you will examine public opinion about civil liberties and civil rights.

♦ EXERCISE 16 ♦

Civil Liberties: Free Speech

Open the **NORC93** data set and select the **Univariate Statistics** function. Use **45** or **ATH. SPEAK** as the variable. *Press* **D** (for Distribution).

Somebody who is against all churches and religion: If such a person wanted to make a speech in your (city/town/community) against churches and religion, should he be allowed to speak, or not?

	FREQUENCY	%
ALLOWED	764	72.5
NOT ALLOWD	290	27.5

Nearly three-fourths of Americans would grant freedom of speech to a militant atheist.

Use **47** or **RACIST SPK** as the variable. *Press* **D** (for Distribution).

If such a person wanted to make a speech in your community claiming that blacks are inferior, should he be allowed to speak, or not?

Exercise 16: Civil Liberties: Free Speech

	FREQUENCY	%
ALLOWED	649	62.0
NOT ALLOWD	397	38.0

Fewer are willing to extend freedom of speech to a racist.

Use **46** or **COMMIE SPK** as the variable. *Press* **D** (for Distribution).

Suppose this admitted Communist wanted to make a speech in your community. Should he be allowed to speak, or not?

	FREQUENCY	%
ALLOWED	736	70.5
NOT ALLOWD	308	29.5

The proportion of Americans who would permit a Communist to speak is about the same as for an atheist.

When social scientists wish to measure a somewhat complex set of attitudes such as these three on freedom of speech, they often use a device called a *scale*. A scale assigns scores to individuals on the basis of their answers to some set of questions—much as people are assigned scores when they take quizzes. In this case, people earned one point for responding ALLOWED to each of these three questions. Thus, people who would extend free speech in all three instances got a score of three on the scale of free speech. People who answered NOT ALLOWED to all three got a score of zero. To simplify the scale, people were assigned to the three categories shown below, depending on their scores.

SCALE CATEGORY	SCORE
HIGH	3
MEDIUM	2
LOW	1–0

Use **48** or **FR. SPEECH** as the variable. *Press* **D** (for Distribution).

	FREQUENCY	%
HIGH	537	52.5
MEDIUM	315	30.8
LOW	170	16.6

All things considered, Americans have considerable respect for freedom of speech—more than half would extend free speech in all three instances.

Switch to the **Tabular Statistics** function and use **48** or **FR. SPEECH** as the row variable and **1** or **PRES IN 92** as the column variable. *Press* **C** for column percentages. This table will appear:

	CLINTON	BUSH	PEROT
HIGH	55.0	49.4	62.5
MEDIUM	29.7	33.1	25.8
LOW	15.3	17.5	11.7

These differences are not significant.

Use **48** or **FR. SPEECH** as the row variable and **85** or **DEM/REP** as the column variable. *Press* **C** for column percentages. This table will appear:

	DEMOCRAT	REPUBLICAN
HIGH	51.2	54.6
MEDIUM	30.4	29.1
LOW	18.4	16.3

There appears to be a tiny party difference, but it is not significant statistically.

Use **48** or **FR. SPEECH** as the row variable and **29** or **WATCH TV** as the column variable. *Press* **C** for column percentages. This table will appear:

	1 OR LESS	TWO	3–4	OVER 4
HIGH	59.8	60.5	47.0	37.9
MEDIUM	25.9	26.6	32.1	43.1
LOW	14.3	12.9	20.9	19.0

The more hours of television that people watch per day, the less likely they are to score high on support for free speech.

But does it matter what they watch? Maybe watching Public Television will increase support for free speech?

Use **48** or **FR. SPEECH** as the row variable and **31** or **TV PBS** as the column variable. *Press* **C** for column percentages. This table will appear:

	DAILY	WEEKLY	MONTHLY	RARELY
HIGH	49.5	55.7	54.9	50.3
MEDIUM	34.2	31.1	25.9	30.9
LOW	16.3	13.3	19.2	18.8

Watching Public Television has no significant effect on support for free speech.

Use **48** or **FR. SPEECH** as the row variable and **17** or **EDUCATION** as the column variable. *Press* **C** for column percentages. This table will appear:

Exercise 16: Civil Liberties: Free Speech

	NOT HS GRAD	HS GRAD	SOME COLL.	COLL GRAD
HIGH	32.5	45.5	57.9	70.0
MEDIUM	38.1	35.1	27.8	23.6
LOW	29.4	19.4	14.3	6.4

Education has a very strong effect upon support for free speech.

Use **48** or **FR. SPEECH** as the row variable and **92** or **OVER 50** as the column variable. *Press* **C** for column percentages. This table will appear:

	UNDER 50	50 OR MORE
HIGH	57.8	43.3
MEDIUM	30.3	31.6
LOW	12.0	25.1

People over 50 are less supportive of free speech than those under 50. Perhaps that is because people over 50 are less likely to have completed high school. To see if that removes the age differences, recreate the table above using the subset function to limit the data to people with less than a high school education (value 1 on variable 17).

SUBSET WITH VALUE NOT HS GRAD

	UNDER 50	50 OR MORE
HIGH	44.8	22.0
MEDIUM	36.8	39.5
LOW	18.4	38.5

No. A highly significant age difference remains among those with little education.

WORKSHEET

NAME:

COURSE:

DATE:

EXERCISE 16

Workbook exercises and software are copyrighted. Copying is prohibited by law.

1. Using the **NORC93** data set and the **Tabular Statistics** function, create and fill in the following table. Row variable: **48** or **FR. SPEECH**; column variable: **6** or **SEX**. (Don't forget to properly percentage your tables!)

	MALE	FEMALE
HIGH	%	%
MEDIUM	%	%
LOW	%	%

Are males or females more apt to score high on support for free speech? (circle one)   MALES   FEMALES   SAME

Is the difference significant? (circle one)   YES   NO

Prob. = _____

What is the value of Cramer's V?   V = _____

2. Create and fill in the following table. Row variable: **45** or **ATH. SPEAK**; column variable: **6** or **SEX**.

	MALE	FEMALE
ALLOWED	%	%
NOT ALLOWD	%	%

Are males or females more apt to allow an atheist to give a speech? (circle one)   MALES   FEMALES   SAME

Is the difference significant? (circle one)   YES   NO

Prob. = _____

What is the value of Cramer's V?   V = _____

Exercise 16: Civil Liberties: Free Speech

WORKSHEET	EXERCISE 16

3. Create and fill in the following table. Row variable: **47** or **RACIST SPK**; column variable: **6** or **SEX**.

	MALE	FEMALE
ALLOWED	%	%
NOT ALLOWD	%	%

Are males or females more apt to allow a racist to give a speech? (circle one)   MALES   FEMALES   SAME

Is the difference significant? (circle one)   YES   NO

Prob. = _____

What is the value of Cramer's V?   V = _____

4. Create and fill in the following table. Row variable: **46** or **COMMIE SPK**; column variable: **6** or **SEX**.

	MALE	FEMALE
ALLOWED	%	%
NOT ALLOWD	%	%

Are males or females more apt to allow a Communist to give a speech? (circle one)   MALES   FEMALES   SAME

Is the difference significant? (circle one)   YES   NO

Prob. = _____

What is the value of Cramer's V?   V = _____

Looking at each of the three specific free speech questions above, for which speaker are gender differences largest? (Compare V values.) _____

5. Why do you think these gender differences exist in support for freedom of speech?

NAME	EXERCISE 16

6. Create and fill in the following table. Row variable: **48** or **FR. SPEECH**; column variable: **8** or **RACE**.

	WHITE	AFRICAN-AM
HIGH	%	%
MEDIUM	%	%
LOW	%	%

Are whites or African Americans more apt to score high on support for free speech? (circle one)   WHITES   AFRICAN-AM   SAME

Is the difference significant? (circle one)   YES   NO

Prob. = _____

What is the value of Cramer's V?   V = _____

7. Create and fill in the following table. Row variable: **45** or **ATH. SPEAK**; column variable: **8** or **RACE**.

	WHITE	AFRICAN-AM
ALLOWED	%	%
NOT ALLOWD	%	%

Are whites or African Americans more apt to allow an atheist to speak? (circle one)   WHITES   AFRICAN-AM   SAME

Is the difference significant? (circle one)   YES   NO

Prob. = _____

What is the value of Cramer's V?   V = _____

8. Create and fill in the following table. Row variable: **47** or **RACIST SPK**; column variable: **8** or **RACE**.

	WHITE	AFRICAN-AM
ALLOWED	%	%
NOT ALLOWD	%	%

Exercise 16: Civil Liberties: Free Speech

| WORKSHEET | EXERCISE 16 |

Are whites or African Americans more apt to allow a racist to speak? (circle one)   WHITES   AFRICAN-AM   SAME

Is the difference significant? (circle one)   YES   NO

Prob. = _____

What is the value of Cramer's V?   V = _____

9. Create and fill in the following table. Row variable: **46** or **COMMIE SPK**; column variable: **8** or **RACE**.

	WHITE	AFRICAN-AM
ALLOWED	%	%
NOT ALLOWD	%	%

Are whites or African Americans more apt to allow a Communist to speak? (circle one)   WHITES   AFRICAN-AM   SAME

Is the difference significant? (circle one)   YES   NO

Prob. = _____

What is the value of Cramer's V?   V = _____

Looking at each of the three specific free speech questions above, for which speaker are racial differences largest? (Compare V values.) _____

♦ OPTIONAL CHALLENGE ASSIGNMENT ♦

Use the **P1973–93** data set and explore changes in support for freedom of speech using the questions about letting Communists or atheists speak. Remember to always use **1** or **YEAR** as the column variable. To see if changes occurred in all age groups, all regions, among both whites and African Americans, political parties, etc., use these (one at a time) as control variables.

Part IV: Freedom

◆ EXERCISE 17 ◆
Civil Rights: Segregation

Open the **NORC93** data set and select the **Univariate Statistics** function. Use **41** or **SEGREGATE?** as the variable. After the graphic appears, *press* **D** (for Distribution).

White people have a right to keep blacks out of their neighborhoods if they want to, and blacks should respect that right.

	FREQUENCY	%
AGREE	151	14.4
DISAGREE	899	85.6

This question lets us see that individual freedom can't be unlimited because too often one person's freedom infringes upon the freedom of someone else. In this case, the freedom of whites to live in an all-white neighborhood would greatly limit where blacks could live. Of course, for a long time that is precisely what happened—whites did restrict where blacks could live. This was referred to as *segregation*.

In addition to forcing blacks to live in black neighborhoods, policies of segregation often forced blacks to attend black movie theaters, to eat only in black restaurants, to attend all-black schools and colleges, and to stay in black hotels. Efforts to end segregation and other racial restrictions became known as the Civil Rights Movement precisely because these limits on black freedoms violated constitutional guarantees of civil rights.

Today, only about one American in seven approves of segregation. However, it is one thing to disapprove of segregation and something else to agree that the rights of property owners should be subordinated to the goal of an integrated society.

Use **42** or **FAIR HOUSE** as the variable. After the graphic appears, *press* **D** (for Distribution).

SELECT FROM A. One law says that a homeowner can decide for himself whom to sell his house to, even if he prefers not to sell to blacks, or B. The second law says that a homeowner cannot refuse to sell to someone because of his or her race or color.

	FREQUENCY	%
UP 2 OWNER	314	31.6
MUST SELL	680	68.4

Nearly a third of Americans think homeowners should be allowed to sell to whomever they wish, even if they are prejudiced.

Switch to the **Tabular Statistics** function and use **41** or **SEGREGATE?** as the row variable and **8** or **RACE** as the column variable. *Press* **C** for column percentages. This table will appear:

	WHITE	AFRICAN-AM
AGREE	15.1	7.3
DISAGREE	84.9	92.7

No one would be surprised that race matters—that whites are twice as likely as African Americans to agree that whites have a right to their own neighborhoods. But many would be surprised at how small the difference is and that even 7 percent of African Americans agree too.

Use **42** or **FAIR HOUSE** as the row variable and **8** or **RACE** as the column variable. *Press* **C** for column percentages. This table will appear:

	WHITE	AFRICAN-AM
UP 2 OWNER	34.7	14.4
MUST SELL	65.3	85.6

Here too racial differences are smaller than might be expected—1 out of 7 African Americans also think homeowners should be able to sell to whomever they wish. This forces us to recognize that not only do some whites wish to live in white neighborhoods, some African Americans wish to live in African-American neighborhoods.

Use **41** or **SEGREGATE?** as the row variable and **48** or **FR. SPEECH** as the column variable. *Press* **C** for column percentages. This table will appear:

	HIGH	MEDIUM	LOW
AGREE	8.3	16.9	27.1
DISAGREE	91.7	83.1	72.9

Here we see that support for civil liberties and support for civil rights tend to go together. People who score low on support for free speech are more than three times as likely as those who score high to agree with the statement advocating segregation. However, even among those low on support for free speech, the great majority reject segregation.

Use **41** or **SEGREGATE?** as the row variable and **85** or **DEM/REP** as the column variable. *Press* **C** for column percentages. This table will appear:

	DEMOCRAT	REPUBLICAN
AGREE	14.5	14.9
DISAGREE	85.5	85.1

Party doesn't matter.

Use **42** or **FAIR HOUSE** as the row variable and **85** or **DEM/REP** as the column variable. *Press* **C** for column percentages. This table will appear:

	DEMOCRAT	REPUBLICAN
UP 2 OWNER	26.4	38.3
MUST SELL	73.6	61.7

But party is modestly related to support for fair housing laws. Before going any farther, however, an experienced political scientist would worry that race was distorting these findings since African Americans are so overwhelmingly Democrats.

So, let's recreate this table using the subset function to limit the data to whites. (As you will recall, this is accomplished by making **8** or **RACE** the subset variable, and making **1** both the lower and the upper limit.) *Press* **C** for column percentages. This table will appear:

SUBSET WITH VALUE WHITE

	DEMOCRAT	REPUBLICAN
UP 2 OWNER	30.2	39.2
MUST SELL	69.8	60.8

The difference between parties is reduced, but it remains significant.

Use **41** or **SEGREGATE?** as the row variable and **1** or **PRES IN 92** as the column variable. *Press* **C** for column percentages. This table will appear:

	CLINTON	BUSH	PEROT
AGREE	12.0	15.6	16.7
DISAGREE	88.0	84.4	83.3

As with party, presidential voting is not significantly related to support for segregation.

Use **42** or **FAIR HOUSE** as the row variable and **1** or **PRES IN 92** as the column variable. *Press* **C** for column percentages. This table will appear:

	CLINTON	BUSH	PEROT
UP 2 OWNER	28.9	39.4	27.4
MUST SELL	71.1	60.6	72.6

But, also like party, voting preferences are significantly related to opinions about fair housing laws.

Use **41** or **SEGREGATE?** as the row variable and **29** or **WATCH TV** as the column variable. *Press* **C** for column percentages. This table will appear:

	1 OR LESS	TWO	3–4	OVER 4
AGREE	10.5	11.8	16.7	20.4
DISAGREE	89.5	88.2	83.3	79.6

The more time per day people spend watching TV the more willing they are to approve of segregation.

Use **29** or **WATCH TV** as the row variable and **8** or **RACE** as the column variable. *Press* **C** for column percentages. This table will appear:

Exercise 17: Civil Rights: Segregation

	WHITE	AFRICAN-AM
1 OR LESS	25.7	14.5
TWO	28.1	26.2
3–4	32.0	30.2
OVER 4	14.2	29.1

There are substantial racial differences in amount of TV viewing. So, it might be wise to examine the impact of TV on segregation attitudes for whites only.

Use **41** or **SEGREGATE?** as the row variable and **29** or **WATCH TV** as the column variable and **8** or **RACE** as the subset variable and make 1 the lower and the upper limit. *Press* **C** for column percentages. This table will appear:

SUBSET WITH VALUE WHITE

	1 OR LESS	TWO	3–4	OVER 4
AGREE	9.5	13.1	17.8	25.0
DISAGREE	90.5	86.9	82.2	75.0

As might be predicted, TV has an even greater effect when the data are limited to whites.

Your turn.

WORKSHEET

NAME:

COURSE:

DATE:

Workbook exercises and software are copyrighted. Copying is prohibited by law.

EXERCISE 17

1. Using the **NORC93** data set and **Tabular Statistics**, create and fill in the following table. Row variable: **41** or **SEGREGATE?**; column variable: **6** or **SEX**. (Remember to provide column percentages for your tables.)

	MALE	FEMALE
AGREE	%	%
DISAGREE	%	%

Are males or females more apt to favor segregation? (circle one)   MALES   FEMALES

Is the difference significant? (circle one)   YES   NO

Prob. = _____

What is the value of Cramer's V?   V = _____

2. Create and fill in the following table. Row variable: **42** or **FAIR HOUSE**; column variable: **6** or **SEX**.

	MALE	FEMALE
UP 2 OWNER	%	%
MUST SELL	%	%

Are males or females more apt to favor fair housing laws? (circle one)   MALES   FEMALES

Is the difference significant? (circle one)   YES   NO

Prob. = _____

What is the value of Cramer's V?   V = _____

Exercise 17: Civil Rights: Segregation

WORKSHEET EXERCISE 17

3. Contrast these findings with those concerning support for free speech in the previous exercise.

4. Create and fill in the following table. Row variable: **41** or **SEGREGATE?**; column variable: **18** or **FAMILY $**.

	UNDER $12K	$12–$23K	$23–$35K	$35–$60K	OVER $60K
AGREE	%	%	%	%	%
DISAGREE	%	%	%	%	%

Are upper- or lower-income families more likely to favor segregation? (circle one)   UPPER   LOWER

Is the difference significant? (circle one)   YES   NO

Prob. = _____

What is the value of Cramer's V?   V = _____

5. Create and fill in the following table. Row variable: **42** or **FAIR HOUSE**; column variable: **18** or **FAMILY $**.

	UNDER $12K	$12–$23K	$23–$35K	$35–$60K	OVER $60K
UP 2 OWNER	%	%	%	%	%
MUST SELL	%	%	%	%	%

Are upper- or lower-income families more likely to favor fair housing laws? (circle one)   UPPER   LOWER

Is the difference significant? (circle one)   YES   NO

Prob. = _____

What is the value of Cramer's V?   V = _____

NAME _____   EXERCISE 17

6. Create and fill in the following table. Row variable: **41** or **SEGREGATE?**; column variable: **90** or **SOUTH/NOT**.

	SOUTH	NON-SOUTH
AGREE	%	%
DISAGREE	%	%

   In which region are people most likely to favor segregation? _____

   Is the difference significant? (circle one)   YES   NO

   Prob. = _____

   What is the value of Cramer's V?   V = _____

7. Now recreate this same table, only using the subset function to limit the data to whites. (Use **8** or **RACE** as the subset variable making **1** the lower and upper limits.)

   SUBSET WITH VALUE WHITE

	SOUTH	NON-SOUTH
AGREE	%	%
DISAGREE	%	%

   In which region are people most likely to favor segregation? _____

   Is the difference significant? (circle one)   YES   NO

   Prob. = _____

   What is the value of Cramer's V?   V = _____

8. Create and fill in the following table. Row variable: **42** or **FAIR HOUSE**; column variable: **90** or **SOUTH/NOT**. Use **8** or **RACE** as the subset variable making **1** the lower and the upper limit, thus limiting the data to whites.

   SUBSET WITH VALUE WHITE

	SOUTH	NON-SOUTH
UP 2 OWNER	%	%
MUST SELL	%	%

Exercise 17: Civil Rights: Segregation

WORKSHEET	EXERCISE 17

In which region are people most likely to favor fair housing laws? _____

Is the difference significant? (circle one)   YES   NO

Prob. = _____

What is the value of Cramer's V?   V = _____

9. Create and fill in the following table. Row variable: **41** or **SEGREGATE**; column variable: **7** or **AGE**.

	18–29	30–39	40–49	50–65	OVER 65
AGREE	%	%	%	%	%
DISAGREE	%	%	%	%	%

In which age group are people most likely to support segregation? _____

In which age group are people least likely to support segregation? _____

Is the difference significant? (circle one)   YES   NO

Prob. = _____

What is the value of Cramer's V?   V = _____

Suppose some political scientists looked at this table and said it was a very encouraging finding. Why might they say that? Would you agree with them? Why or why not?

♦ OPTIONAL CHALLENGE ASSIGNMENT ♦

Using the **P1973–93** data set, explore changes in opposition to interracial marriage and/or support for fair housing laws.

PART V

FOREIGN AFFAIRS

This final exercise will focus on foreign affairs and on voter support for the government taking an active role in world affairs.

◆ EXERCISE 18 ◆

America's Role in the World

Open the **NORC93** data set and select the **Univariate Statistics** function. Use **76** or **US ACTIVE** as the variable. After the graphic appears, *press* **D** (for Distribution).

Do you think it will be best for the future of this country if we take an active part in world affairs, or if we stay out of world affairs?

	FREQUENCY	%
ACTIVE	725	70.3
STAY OUT	306	29.7

The majority of Americans think it would be better for the future of the country if we take an active part in world affairs.

But what do people think it means for the nation to take an active role in world affairs? Perhaps it means leaving the UN: *Do you think our government should continue to belong to the United Nations or should we pull out?*

Go to the **Tabular Statistics** function and use **77** or **OUT OF UN?** as the row variable and **76** or **US ACTIVE** as the column variable. When the table appears, *press* **C** for column percentages. These results will appear:

	ACTIVE	STAY OUT	TOTAL
STAY	95.9	73.8	89.6
GET OUT	4.1	26.2	10.4

For some people (26.2%), staying out of world affairs would include dropping out of the UN. But the total column shows that only about 1 American in 10 thinks we should leave the UN.

Use **78** or **FOREIGN $** as the row variable and **76** or **US ACTIVE** as the column variable. *Press* **C** for column percentages. This table will appear:

Exercise 18: America's Role in the World

	ACTIVE	STAY OUT	TOTAL
TOO MUCH	73.6	75.8	74.3
ABOUT RITE	26.4	24.2	25.7

However, those who favor our active involvement in the world are not more willing to spend money on foreign aid—3 out of 4 Americans think too much is being spent on foreign aid. So few thought we were spending too little that no such category needed to be provided.

Use **79** or **DEFENSE $** as the row variable and **76** or **US ACTIVE** as the column variable. *Press* **C** for column percentages. This table will appear:

	ACTIVE	STAY OUT	TOTAL
TOO MUCH	42.9	44.4	43.3
ABOUT RITE	57.1	55.6	56.7

Nor would they seem inclined to raise military spending to sustain our active role in world affairs. Perhaps many people do not think an active role would involve military action: *Do you expect the United States to fight in another world war within the next ten years?*

Use **80** or **WAR IN 10Y** as the row variable and **76** or **US ACTIVE** as the column variable. *Press* **C** for column percentages. This table will appear:

	ACTIVE	STAY OUT	TOTAL
YES	39.9	68.1	48.4
NO	60.1	31.9	51.6

Here we may gain a major insight into the issue of America's role in the world. The great majority of those who want us to be active do not anticipate our involvement in a major war in the next 10 years—perhaps they think war can be prevented by our active involvement. In contrast, the great majority (68.1%) of those who want us to stay out of world affairs do expect war within 10 years—perhaps they fear that by being active in world affairs we will be drawn into a war which we could avoid by going our own way.

Use **76** or **US ACTIVE** as the row variable and **85** or **DEM/REP** as the column variable. *Press* **C** for column percentages. This table will appear:

	DEMOCRAT	REPUBLICAN
ACTIVE	67.9	74.2
STAY OUT	32.1	25.8

Most of the supporters of each party favor America taking an active role, but Republicans are significantly, but only slightly, more likely than Democrats to take this position.

Use **76** or **US ACTIVE** as the row variable and **23** or **REGION** as the column variable. *Press* **C** for column percentages. This table will appear:

	EAST	MIDWEST	SOUTH	WEST
ACTIVE	76.7	76.4	66.1	70.5
STAY OUT	23.3	23.6	33.9	29.5

There are no significant regional differences.

Use **76** or **US ACTIVE** as the row variable and **6** or **SEX** as the column variable. *Press* **C** for column percentages. This table will appear:

	MALE	FEMALE
ACTIVE	74.1	67.2
STAY OUT	25.9	32.8

Women are a bit less likely than men to support an active role for the United States. Let's follow this up.

Use **80** or **WAR IN 10Y** as the row variable and **6** or **SEX** as the column variable. *Press* **C** for column percentages. This table will appear:

	MALE	FEMALE
YES	38.7	56.6
NO	61.3	43.4

Women are far more worried about a major war in 10 years than are men. Let's see if lack of confidence in the military influences these gender differences.

Use **80** or **WAR IN 10Y** as the row variable and **6** or **SEX** as the column variable and **60** or **MILITARY?** as the control variable. This will create three tables: one for those with a great deal of confidence in the military, one for those with only some confidence, and one for those with hardly any confidence in the military. If women are more apt to expect a war *because* they lack confidence in the military, then the gender differences ought to disappear among those with similar levels of confidence.

The first table to appear will be for those having a great deal of confidence. (*Press* **C** for column percentages for each table.)

GREAT DEAL

	MALE	FEMALE
YES	41.5	59.0
NO	58.5	41.0

A significant gender difference remains in this table. *Press* <ENTER> to move on to the second table.

ONLY SOME

	MALE	FEMALE
YES	43.8	61.5
NO	56.2	38.5

Exercise 18: America's Role in the World

Here too the difference is significant. *Press <ENTER> again* to move to the third table.

HARDLY ANY

	MALE	FEMALE
YES	24.0	72.7
NO	76.0	27.3

And even here where the number of cases is small, the difference is significant. Thus, lack of confidence in military does not explain the gender difference.

Now switch to the **P1973–93** data set and go back to the **Tabular Statistics** task. Use **9** or **STAY IN UN** as the row variable and **1** or **YEAR** as the column variable. *Press* **C** for column percentages. This table will appear:

	1973	**1993**
STAY IN	84.1	89.7
PULL OUT	15.9	10.3

There has been a small, but statistically significant, increase in public support for remaining in the UN.

Should you care to do so, you can discover that there has been no significant change in support for spending on defense or foreign aid.

WORKSHEET

NAME:

COURSE:

DATE:

EXERCISE 18

Workbook exercises and software are copyrighted. Copying is prohibited by law.

1. Using the **NORC93** data set and the **Tabular Statistics** function, create and fill in the following table. Use **76** or **US ACTIVE** as the row variable and **7** or **AGE** as the column variable. (Remember to use column percentaging in all of the tables throughout this exercise.)

	18–29	30–39	40–49	50–65	OVER 65
ACTIVE	%	%	%	%	%
STAY OUT	%	%	%	%	%

In which age group is there the least support for the United States taking an active part in world affairs? _____

Is the difference significant? (circle one)   YES   NO

Prob. = _____

2. Create and fill in the following table. Row variable: **80** or **WAR IN 10Y**; column variable: **7** or **AGE**.

	18–29	30–39	40–49	50–65	OVER 65
YES	%	%	%	%	%
NO	%	%	%	%	%

In which age group is there the largest percentage who expect war within 10 years? _____

Is the difference significant? (circle one)   YES   NO

Prob. = _____

Exercise 18: America's Role in the World

WORKSHEET	EXERCISE 18

3. Looking at these two tables, how would you explain these particular age patterns?

4. Create and fill in the following table. Row variable: **80** or **WAR IN 10Y**; column variable: **15** or **VETERAN?**.

	VETERAN	NON-VET
YES	%	%
NO	%	%

Are veterans or non-veterans more apt to expect war in the next 10 years? (circle one)   VETERANS   NON-VETS

Is the difference significant? (circle one)   YES   NO

Prob. = _____

5. Recreate the table above, but use **6** or **SEX** as the subset variable with **1** as the lower and the upper limits in order to examine men only.

	VETERAN	NON-VET
YES	%	%
NO	%	%

Is the difference significant? (circle one)   YES   NO

Prob. = _____

6. Create and fill in the following table. Row variable: **80** or **WAR IN 10Y**; column variable: **8** or **RACE**.

	WHITE	AFRICAN-AM
YES	%	%
NO	%	%

Part V: Foreign Affairs

NAME _____   EXERCISE 18

Are whites or African Americans more apt to expect war in the next 10 years? (circle one)   WHITES   AFRICAN-AM

Is the difference significant? (circle one)   YES   NO

Prob. = _____

7. Create and fill in the following table. Row variable: **76** or **US ACTIVE**; column variable: **28** or **READ PAPER**.

	DAILY	WEEKLY	SELDOM
ACTIVE	%	%	%
STAY OUT	%	%	%

Which group is most likely to support an active role in world affairs? _____

Which group is least likely to support an active role in world affairs? _____

Are the differences significant? (circle one)   YES   NO

Prob. = _____

8. Create and fill in the following table. Row variable: **80** or **WAR IN 10Y**; column variable: **28** or **READ PAPER**.

	DAILY	WEEKLY	SELDOM
YES	%	%	%
NO	%	%	%

Which group is most likely to expect war in the next 10 years? _____

Which group is least likely to expect war in the next 10 years? _____

Are the differences significant? (circle one)   YES   NO

Prob. = _____

Exercise 18: America's Role in the World

| WORKSHEET | | | | EXERCISE 18 |

9. Create and fill in the following table. Row variable: **80** or **WAR IN 10Y**; column variable: **29** or **WATCH TV**.

	1 OR LESS	TWO	3–4	OVER 4
YES	%	%	%	%
NO	%	%	%	%

Which group is most likely to expect war in the next 10 years? _____

Which group is least likely to expect war in the next 10 years? _____

Are the differences significant? (circle one)   YES   NO

Prob. = _____

10. Suggest an explanation for these differences between the two news sources.

♦ OPTIONAL CHALLENGE ASSIGNMENT ♦

Use the **NORC93** data set and explore how liking or disliking Japan (the column variable) influences attitudes about America's role in world affairs and the expectation of war. And what influences liking of Japan (using it as the row variable)? Do the same results appear when liking Israel is substituted?

APPENDIX A

INDEPENDENT PROJECTS

There are many variables in these data files that have been little used or not used at all. Many of these could provide the basis for an independent research project. Such projects need not be limited to this course or even to other courses in political science. You could use your research findings as the basis for papers in other social science courses or even in writing or communications courses.

The following suggestions may help you identify some suitable projects.

◆ CAPITAL PUNISHMENT ◆

NORC93: 50 or **EXECUTE?**: *Do you favor or oppose the death penalty for persons convicted of murder?*

FAVOR	77.4%
OPPOSE	22.6%

P1973–93: 21 or **EXECUTE** (same wording. Big shift to favor).

FIFTY: 6 or **CAP.PUNISH**: *which states have the death penalty.*

Race is a key variable in both survey data files. Also check out party.

◆ GUN CONTROL ◆

NORC93: 51 or **GUN CONTRL**: *Would you favor or oppose a law which would require a person to obtain a police permit before he or she could buy a gun?*

FAVOR	82.5%
OPPOSE	17.5%

P1973–93: 20 or **GUN CONTROL** (same wording).

HOUSE: 27 or **GUN BILL**: *Vote on the so-called Brady Bill, which requires a five-day waiting period for handgun purchases.*

SENATE: 24 or **GUN CONTRL**: Same as House

You will discover interesting things when you use sex, party, gun ownership, and region.

Independent Projects

♦ SUICIDE ♦

Dr. Jack Kevorkian has made assisted suicide into a major political issue. But there has been surprisingly little in the press on how the general public views suicide, even though the question below has appeared in the GSS for the past few years.

NORC93: 69 or **SUIC.WISH**: *Person has the right to end own life if this person is tired of living and ready to die?*

YES	16.1%
NO	83.9%

FIFTY: 44 or **SUICIDE**: *Rate of suicides per 100,000 population.*

Religion and region are very important.

♦ ANIMAL RIGHTS ♦

Animal rights issues have entered the political arena as activists have posed naked to protest wearing fur or have broken into medical laboratories to "free" laboratory animals.

NORC93: 70 or **ANIM.RIGHT**: *Animals should have the same moral rights that human beings do.*

AGREE	31.9%
DISAGREE	68.1%

71 or **ANIM.TEST**: *It is right to use animals for medical testing if it might save human lives.*

AGREE	31.9%
UNCERTAIN	14.5%
DISAGREE	68.1%

There is a quite interesting pattern to be found by seeing how abortion attitudes are and are not related to animal rights attitudes. The relationships between these animal rights items and the vegetarian item (**75**) also are of interest.

♦ ENVIRONMENTALISM ♦

NORC93: 72 or **GREEN TAX**: *And how willing would you be to pay much higher taxes in order to protect the environment?*

WILLING	40.2%
UNWILLING	59.8%

73 or GREEN CUT: *And how willing would you be to accept cuts in your standard of living in order to protect the environment?*

WILLING	34.1%
UNWILLING	65.9%

74 or GREEN DIF: *It is just too difficult for someone like me to do much about the environment.*

AGREE	25.7%
NEITHER	14.0%
DISAGREE	60.3%

P1973–93: 6 or ENVIRON $: *Spending on improving and protecting the environment.*

There has been a slight downward shift in willingness to spend.

◆ MUSIC AND POLITICS ◆

During his campaign, Bill Clinton appeared several times on MTV playing his saxophone. A number of questions about musical tastes appeared in the 1993 GSS. Why not use them to see if music has a distinct political beat?

NORC93: 33 or COUNTRY&W.: *Like Country and Western music*

LIKES	62.1%
MIXES	23.1%
DISLIKES	14.8%

34 or BIG BAND: *Big band (Swing) music*

LIKES	59.9%
MIXES	20.3%
DISLIKES	19.8%

36 or POP/ROCK: *Pop/Rock music*

LIKES	55.1%
MIXES	19.2%
DISLIKES	25.7%

Independent Projects

35 or **CLASSICAL**: *Classical music*

LIKES	49.6%
MIXES	24.3%
DISLIKES	26.1%

37 or **RAP MUSIC**: *Rap music*

LIKES	13.2%
MIXES	18.5%
DISLIKES	68.3%

38 or **HEAVY METL**: *Heavy Metal music*

LIKES	11.2%
MIXES	12.4%
DISLIKES	76.4%

You probably will be quite surprised by how these musical variables relate to party and vote. But the really interesting findings arise when musical tastes are related to "cultural" politics such as vegetarianism, animal rights, environmentalism, abortion, suicide, and capital punishment. Pay particular attention to Heavy Metal music.

APPENDIX B

CODEBOOKS

Note: Additional variables may have been added after publication. Use the **F3** key to view these variables at the end of the file.

◆ SHORT LABEL: ANES92 ◆

1) VOTE? 92
2) PRES IN 92
3) WHO IN 88
4) INTEREST?
5) CARE WINS?
6) PARTY?
7) IDEOLOGY
8) INFORMED?
9) TV NEWS?
10) TV PREZ
11) READ PAPER
12) TALK SHOWS
13) ON SOC SEC
14) FD. STAMPS
15) MEDICARE?
16) MEDICAID?
17) ON UNEMPL.
18) ON AFDC?
19) RAISE TAX?
20) DRAFT
21) UNIONIZED?
22) FAMILY $
23) LATE PAY?
24) CATH/PROT
25) CH.ATTEND
26) AGE
27) MARITAL
28) EDUCATION
29) WH/AFRIC.A
30) SEX
31) REGION

◆ SHORT LABEL: FIFTY ◆

1) Case ID
2) FED FUNDS
3) %FED LAND
4) FED.EMPLOY
5) DEFENSE $
6) CAP.PUNISH
7) STATES '92
8) %CLINTON92
9) %BUSH '92
10) %PEROT 92
11) STATES1988
12) %BUSH 1988
13) STATES '84
14) %REAGAN 84
15) STATES '72
16) %NIXON '72
17) STATES '64
18) %JOHNSON64
19) STATES '60
20) %KENNEDY60
21) STATES '20
22) %HARDING20
23) % LEFT '20
24) STATE 1860
25) %LINCOLN60
26) %BRECKEN60
27) %SLAVE '60
28) % VOTED'92
29) %VOTED '88
30) %VOTED '80
31) %REGIST.92
32) %REGIST.88
33) F.LEGIS.93
34) BLACK LEGL
35) LOBBYISTS
36) VETERANS
37) N.REV./NAT
38) PEACE CORP
39) % JEWISH
40) % CATHOLIC
41) % BAPTIST
42) CH.MEMBERS
43) ABORTIONS
44) SUICIDE
45) PICKUPS
46) FLD&STREAM
47) PLAYBOY
48) GOURMET
49) % WHITE
50) % BLACK
51) % ASIAN
52) % NAT.AMER
53) % HISPANIC
54) % OVER 65
55) AVER. AGE
56) % METROPOL
57) DENSITY
58) $PER CAP.
59) FOODSTAMPS
60) % UNEMPLOY
61) % POOR
62) %MALE HOME
63) % SINGLE
64) MATH SCORE
65) DROPOUTS
66) KINKO'S
67) % WINE
68) % BEER
69) COSMO
70) PLASTIC MD
71) SHRINKS
72) HUNTING
73) TV DISHES
74) COKE USERS
75) MURDER

◆ SHORT LABEL: HOUSE ◆

1) NAME
2) STATE
3) REGION
4) POSITION
5) RACE/ETHNI
6) WH/AF/HI
7) RELIGION
8) RELIGION 3
9) PARTY
10) SOUTH DEM
11) AGE
12) SEX
13) EDUCATION
14) MARITAL
15) LAWYER?
16) NEWCOMERS
17) # TERMS
18) % AFRI-AM.
19) %HISPANIC
20) FAM.INCOME
21) LEAD.LIMIT
22) NO PROXIES
23) TAX UP 3/5
24) UNFUND.MAN
25) UNF.MAN.2
26) LINE VETO
27) DEATH PEN1
28) NAT.SECUR.
29) HLTH DEDUC
30) MINOR.PREF
31) DEFENSE SP
32) RISK ASSES
33) REG.OVER.
34) TAX CUT
35) PROD.LIAB.
36) REG.MORAT
37) DEATH PEN2
38) EXCLUS.RUL
39) PROP.RGTS1
40) LEADER 103
41) % PAC $
42) $ PER VOTE
43) CAMPAIGN $
44) % VOTE
45) TERM LIMIT

◆ SHORT LABEL: NORC93 ◆

1) PRES IN 92
2) PRES.88?
3) VOTE 92?
4) PARTY
5) LIB./CONS.
6) SEX
7) AGE
8) RACE
9) MARITAL
10) #CHILDREN
11) # SIBLINGS
12) RELIGION
13) CH.ATTEND
14) SCH.PRAYER
15) VETERAN?
16) OCC. PREST
17) EDUCATION
18) FAMILY $
19) EVER UNEMP
20) UNIONIZED?
21) HAPPY?
22) DWELLING
23) REGION
24) REG. AT 16
25) PAR. BORN?
26) GUN OWNER?
27) HUNTER?
28) READ PAPER
29) WATCH TV
30) TV NEWS
31) TV PBS
32) CAR RACES?
33) COUNTRY&W.
34) BIG BAND
35) CLASSICAL
36) POP/ROCK
37) RAP MUSIC
38) HEAVY METL
39) WOMAN PREZ
40) MEN BETTER
41) SEGREGATE?
42) FAIR HOUSE
43) BUSING
44) BLACK PREZ
45) ATH. SPEAK
46) COMMIE SPK
47) RACIST SPK
48) FR. SPEECH
49) TAX 2 HIGH
50) EXECUTE?
51) GUN CONTRL
52) COURTS
53) WIRE TAP
54) EX.BRANCH
55) LABOR?
56) PRESS?
57) SCIENCE
58) SUP.COURT
59) CONGRESS?
60) MILITARY?
61) BIG BIZ?
62) EDUCATIONC
63) DEFECT
64) UNWANTED
65) MOM HEALTH
66) UNWED
67) ABORTION
68) PORN.LAW?
69) SUIC.WISH
70) ANIM.RIGHT
71) ANIM.TEST
72) GREEN TAX
73) GREEN CUT
74) GREEN DIF
75) VEGGIE?
76) US ACTIVE
77) OUT OF UN?
78) FOREIGN $
79) DEFENSE $
80) WAR IN 10Y
81) COMMUNISM
82) JAPAN
83) CANADA
84) ISRAEL
85) DEM/REP
86) CATH/PROT
87) OVER TAXED
88) WELFARE $
89) POOR $
90) SOUTH/NOT
91) COLLEGE/NT
92) OVER 50
93) OVER 30

◆ SHORT LABEL: OLDHOUSE ◆

1) NAME
2) STATE
3) REGION
4) POSITION
5) RACE/ETHNI
6) WH/AF/HI
7) RELIGION
8) RELIGION 3
9) PARTY
10) SOUTH DEM
11) AGE
12) SEX
13) LEADER
14) # TERMS
15) ADA 1993
16) CAMPAIGN $
17) $ PER VOTE
18) % PAC $

◆ SHORT LABEL: OLDSEN ◆

1) NAME
2) STATE
3) REGION
4) PARTY
5) SOUTH DEM
6) SEX
7) RACE
8) EDUCATION
9) AGE
10) RELIGION
11) MARRIED
12) LAWYER
13) VETERAN
14) TENURE
15) % VOTE
16) CAMPAIGN $
17) $ PER VOTE
18) % OUTSTATE
19) % PAC $
20) ADA 1993
21) FAM.LEAVE
22) HIV IMMIG.
23) CLIN.BUDG
24) GUN CONTRL
25) NAFTA

◆ SHORT LABEL: P1973–93 ◆

1) YEAR
2) RACE
3) REGION
4) AGE
5) PARTY
6) ENVIRON $
7) DEFENSE $
8) FOR. AID$
9) STAY IN UN
10) ATH. SPEAK
11) COMMIE.SPK
12) BIG BIZ?
13) EX.BRANCH
14) PRESS
15) SCIENCE
16) CONGRESS
17) MILITARY
18) INTERMARRY
19) FAIR HOUSE
20) GUN CONTRL
21) EXECUTE

◆ SHORT LABEL: SENATE ◆

1) NAME
2) STATE
3) REGION
4) PARTY
5) SOUTH DEM.
6) SEX
7) RACE/ETH
8) AGE
9) RELIGION
10) EDUCATION
11) MARITAL
12) LAWYER?
13) NEWCOMER?
14) REELECT96?
15) ACCOUNTBLE
16) PAY CUTS
17) UNFUND.MAN
18) BAL.BUDG.
19) LINE VETO
20) RELIGION 3
21) %PAC $
22) $ PER VOTE
23) CAMPAIGN $

♦ LONG LABEL: ANES92 ♦

1) VOTE? 92
Did you vote for a candidate for President?

2) PRES IN 92
Who did you vote for?

3) WHO IN 88
RESPONDENTS VOTE FOR PRESIDENT IN 1988

4) INTEREST?
RESPONDENT'S LEVEL OF INTEREST IN THE CAMPAIGN

5) CARE WINS?
[DO] YOU PERSONALLY CARE A GOOD DEAL WHO WINS THE PRESIDENTIAL ELECTION THIS FALL, OR DON'T YOU CARE VERY MUCH WHO WINS?

6) PARTY?
GENERALLY SPEAKING, DO YOU USUALLY THINK OF YOURSELF AS A REPUBLICAN, DEMOCRAT, INDEPENDENT, OR WHAT?

7) IDEOLOGY
IF YOU HAD TO CHOOSE WOULD YOU CONSIDER YOURSELF A LIBERAL, OR CONSERVATIVE?

8) INFORMED?
INTERVIEWER RATING OF THE RESPONDENT'S GENERAL LEVEL OF INFORMATION ABOUT POLITICS

9) TV NEWS?
HOW MANY DAYS IN THE PAST WEEK DID YOU WATCH THE NEWS ON TV?

10) TV PREZ
HOW MUCH ATTENTION DID YOU PAY TO NEWS ON TV ABOUT THE CAMPAIGN FOR PRESIDENT?

11) READ PAPER
HOW OFTEN DO YOU READ A DAILY NEWSPAPER?

12) TALK SHOWS
DO YOU LISTEN TO OR WATCH SHOWS ON RADIO OR TV WHERE PEOPLE CALL IN TO VOICE THEIR OPINIONS?

13) ON SOC SEC
SOCIAL SECURITY RECIPIENT?

14) FD. STAMPS
FOOD STAMP RECIPIENT

15) MEDICARE?
MEDICARE RECIPIENT

16) MEDICAID?
MEDICAID RECIPIENT?

17) ON UNEMPL.
CURRENTLY ON UNEMPLOYMENT?

18) ON AFDC?
RECIPIENT OF AID TO FAMILIES WITH DEPENDENT CHILDREN?

19) RAISE TAX?
WHICH CANDIDATE FOR PRESIDENT WOULD BE MORE LIKELY TO TRY TO RAISE TAXES?

20) DRAFT
DO YOU THINK THAT MOST MEN WHO TRIED TO AVOID MILITARY SERVICE DURING THE VIETNAM WAR SHOULD HAVE SERVED REGARDLESS OF THEIR PERSONAL BELIEFS?

21) UNIONIZED?
DOES RESPONDENT OR SPOUSE BELONG TO A LABOR UNION?

22) FAMILY $
ANNUAL FAMILY INCOME

23) LATE PAY?
IN THE PAST YEAR HAVE YOU FALLEN BEHIND IN RENT OR HOUSE PAYMENTS?

24) CATH/PROT
RESPONDENT'S RELIGIOUS PREFERENCE:CATHOLICS & PROTESTANTS ONLY

25) CH.ATTEND
FREQUENCY OF CHURCH ATTENDANCE

26) AGE
RESPONDENT'S AGE

27) MARITAL
MARITAL STATUS

28) EDUCATION
RESPONDENT'S EDUCATION

29) WH/AFRIC.A
IS RESPONDENT WHITE OR AFRICAN-AMERICAN?

30) SEX
RESPONDENT'S GENDER

31) REGION
CENSUS REGION

◆ LONG LABEL: FIFTY ◆

1) Case ID

2) FED FUNDS
1989–1991: NET GAIN OR LOSS OF FEDERAL FUNDS: 1.00 = RECEIVED BACK AS MUCH $ AS SENT TO WASHINGTON. LESS THAN 1.00 = NET LOSS; MORE THAN 1.00 = NET GAIN. (VSAP)

3) %FED LAND
1990: PERCENT OF STATE'S AREA THAT IS OWNED BY THE FEDERAL GOV'T. (SR)

4) FED.EMPLOY
1991: NUMBER OF FEDERAL CIVILIAN EMPLOYEES IN EACH STATE PER 100,000 STATE POPULATION (SR)

5) DEFENSE $
1991: DEFENSE DEPT. EXPENDITURES PER CAPITA IN EACH STATE (SR)

6) CAP.PUNISH
1993: DOES STATE HAVE CAPITAL PUNISHMENT? 2 = YES; 1= NO (VSAP)

7) STATES '92
1992: DARK STATES WON BY CLINTON, LIGHT STATES BY BUSH

8) %CLINTON92
1992: PERCENT OF VOTES FOR CLINTON (DEM.)

9) %BUSH '92
1992: PERCENT OF THE VOTES FOR BUSH (REP.)

10) %PEROT 92
1992: PERCENT OF VOTES FOR PEROT (INDEP.)

11) STATES1988
1988: DARK STATES CARRIED BY BUSH (REP.), LIGHT ONES BY DUKAKIS (DEM.)

12) %BUSH 1988
1988: PERCENT OF TWO-PARTY VOTE WON BY GEORGE BUSH (REPUBLICAN)

13) STATES '84
1984: DARK STATES CARRIED BY REAGAN (REP.), LIGHT ONE CARRIED BY MONDALE (DEM.)

14) %REAGAN 84
1984: PERCENT VOTING FOR RONALD REAGAN (REPUBLICAN)

15) STATES '72
1972: DARK STATES WON BY NIXON (REP.), LIGHT ONE BY MCGOVERN (DEM.)

16) %NIXON '72
1972: PERCENT VOTING FOR RICHARD M. NIXON (REPUBLICAN)

17) STATES '64
1964: DARK STATES CARRIED BY JOHNSON (DEM.), LIGHT ONES BY GOLDWATER (REP.)

18) %JOHNSON64
1964: PERCENT VOTING FOR LYNDON B. JOHNSON (DEMOCRAT)

19) STATES '60
1960: DARK STATES WON BY KENNEDY (DEM.), LIGHT BY NIXON (REP.)

20) %KENNEDY60
1960: PERCENT VOTING FOR JOHN F. KENNEDY (DEMOCRAT)

21) STATES '20
1920: DARK STATES CARRIED BY HARDING, LIGHT STATES BY COX

22) %HARDING20
1920: % POPULAR VOTE CAST FOR WARREN G. HARDING (REPUBLICAN)

23) % LEFT '20
1920: % POPULAR VOTE CAST FOR SOCIALIST AND FOR FARMER-LABOR PARTY PRESIDENTIAL CANDIDATES

24) STATE 1860
ELECT.VOTE IN 1860: LINCOLN 3; DOUGLAS 2; BELL 1; BRECKEN. 0

25) %LINCOLN60
1860: PERCENT OF POPULAR VOTE WON BY LINCOLN

26) %BRECKEN60
1860: PERCENT OF POPULAR VOTE CAST FOR BRECKENRIDGE (A.S. 1888)

27) %SLAVE '60
1860: PERCENT OF POPULATION WHO ARE SLAVES (CENSUS, 1860)

28) % VOTED'92
1992: PERCENT OF VOTING AGE POPULATION WHO VOTED IN PRESIDENTIAL ELECTION

29) %VOTED '88
1988: PERCENT OF VOTING AGE POPULATION WHO VOTED IN PRESIDENTIAL ELECTION

30) %VOTED '80
1980: PERCENT OF VOTING AGE POPULATION WHO VOTED IN THE PRESIDENTIAL ELECTION

31) %REGIST.92
1992: PERCENT REGISTERED TO VOTE (N.Dak. & Wisc. don't have registration)

32) %REGIST.88
1988: PERCENT OF VOTING AGE POPULATION REGISTERED TO VOTE. N.Dakota and Wisconsin don't have registration.

33) F.LEGIS.93
1993: PERCENT WOMEN IN STATE LEGISLATURES (from the Center for the American Woman and Politics)

34) BLACK LEGL
1993: PERCENTAGE OF BLACKS IN THE STATE LEGISLATURE (VSAP)

35) LOBBYISTS
1991: NUMBER OF REGISTERED LOBBYISTS PER STATE LEGISLATOR (S.R.)

36) VETERANS
1988: VETERANS PER 1,000 POPULATION (S.A.1990)

37) N.REV./NAT
1990: NATIONAL REVIEW CIRCULATION PER SUBSCRIBER TO THE NATION (ABC)

38) PEACE CORP
1985: TOTAL RESIDENTS WHO JOINED PEACE CORPS 1961–1985 PER 10,000 (THE PEACE CORPS, IN USA TODAY:10/8/85)

39) % JEWISH
1990: PERCENT OF THE POPULATION WHO GIVE THEIR RELIGIOUS PREFERENCES AS JEWISH (KOSMIN)

40) % CATHOLIC
PERCENT OF POPULATION WHO ARE ROMAN CATHOLICS (CHURCH)

41) % BAPTIST
PERCENT OF POPULATION WHO ARE BAPTISTS (CHURCH)

42) CH.MEMBERS
1990: PERCENT OF POPULATION BELONGING TO A LOCAL CHURCH (CHURCH)

43) ABORTIONS
1988: ABORTIONS PER 1,000 LIVE BIRTHS (S.A., 1991)

44) SUICIDE
1989: SUICIDES PER 100,000 (MVSR 1/7/92)

45) PICKUPS
1989: LIGHT TRUCKS (PICKUPS) PER 1,000 (HIGHWAY STATISTICS, 1989)

46) FLD&STREAM
1990: CIRCULATION OF FIELD & STREAM MAGAZINE PER 100,000 (ABC)

47) PLAYBOY
1990: PLAYBOY CIRCULATION PER 100,000 POPULATION (ABC)

48) GOURMET
1990: CIRCULATION OF GOURMET MAGAZINE PER 100,000 (ABC)

49) % WHITE
1990: PERCENT WHITE (CENSUS)

50) % BLACK
1990: PERCENT BLACK (CENSUS)

51) % ASIAN
1990: PERCENT ASIAN (CENSUS)

52) % NAT.AMER
1990: PERCENT NATIVE AMERICAN (CENSUS)

53) % HISPANIC
1990: PERCENT HISPANIC—HISPANICS MAY BE OF ANY RACE (CENSUS)

54) % OVER 65
1990: PERCENT OF THE POPULATION OVER AGE 65 (CENSUS)

55) AVER. AGE
1990: AVERAGE (MEAN) AGE OF THE POPULATION (CENSUS)

56) % METROPOL
1988: PERCENT OF THE POPULATION LIVING IN METROPOLITAN STATISTICAL AREAS (S.A.,1990)

57) DENSITY
1990: POPULATION PER SQUARE MILE (CENSUS)

58) $PER CAP.
1990: PER CAPITA INCOME (S.A., 1991)

59) FOODSTAMPS
1990: PERCENT OF POPULATION RECEIVING FOOD STAMPS (S.P.R., 1991)

60) % UNEMPLOY
1991: PERCENT OF CIVILIAN LABOR FORCE UNEMPLOYED (E&E,11/91)

61) % POOR
1990: PERCENT OF POPULATION BELOW OFFICIAL POVERTY LINE (CENSUS)

62) %MALE HOME
1990: PERCENT OF HOUSEHOLDS WITHOUT AN ADULT FEMALE RESIDENT (CENSUS)

63) % SINGLE
1990: PERCENT OF PERSONS 15 AND OVER WHO HAVE NEVER BEEN MARRIED (CENSUS)

64) MATH SCORE
1991: AVERAGE MATH PROFICIENCY SCORES BY 8TH GRADERS (USA TODAY:6/7/91)

65) DROPOUTS
1990: PERCENT OF PERSONS WHO LEFT SCHOOL WITHOUT GRADUATING FROM HIGH SCHOOL (WA, 1993)

66) KINKO'S
1989: KINKO'S COPY CENTERS PER 100,000 POPULATION (KINKO'S, INC.)

67) % WINE
1989: THE PERCENT OF ALCOHOLIC BEVERAGES CONSUMED THAT WAS WINE (HCSR, 1993)

68) % BEER
1989: THE PERCENTAGE OF ALCOHOLIC BEVERAGES CONSUMED THAT WAS BEER (HCSR, 1993)

69) COSMO
1990: CIRCULATION OF COSMOPOLITAN MAGAZINE PER 100,000 (ABC)

70) PLASTIC MD
1990: PLASTIC SURGEONS PER 100,000 (HCSR, 1993)

71) SHRINKS
1990: NUMBER OF PSYCHIATRISTS PER 100,000 (HCSR, 1993)

72) HUNTING
1990: NUMBER OF RESIDENTS WHO PURCHASED HUNTING LICENSES PER 1,000 POPULATION (U.S.FISH & WILDLIFE)

73) TV DISHES
1990: SATELLITE TV DISHES PER 10,000 (ORBIT MAG. 3/1991)

74) COKE USERS
1990: COCAINE ADDICTS PER 1,000 POPULATION (SENATE JUDICIARY COMMITTEE, USA TODAY:8/6/90)

75) MURDER
1990: MURDERS PER 100,000 (UCR, 1991)

◆ LONG LABEL: HOUSE ◆

1) NAME
Representative's name

2) STATE
Representative's state

3) REGION
REGION

4) POSITION
NUMBER OF STATE POSITION

5) RACE/ETHNI
RACE OR ETHNICITY

6) WH/AF/HI
RACE OR ETHNICITY

7) RELIGION
RELIGIOUS PREFERENCE

8) RELIGION 3
RELIGIOUS PREFERENCE: OTHER OMITTED

9) PARTY
PARTY MEMBERSHIP

10) SOUTH DEM
PARTY WITH DEMOCRATS SEPARATED INTO SOUTHERN AND NON-SOUTHERN

11) AGE
AGE OF REPRESENTATIVE

12) SEX
GENDER

13) EDUCATION
EDUCATION

14) MARITAL
CURRENT MARITAL STATUS

15) LAWYER?
IS MEMBER A LAWYER?

16) NEWCOMERS
WAS PERSON A NEW REPRESENTIVE OR RE-ELECTED?

17) # TERMS
NUMBER OF TERMS SERVED IN THE HOUSE

18) % AFRI-AM.
PERCENT AFRICAN-AMERICAN OF DISTRICT POPULATION

19) %HISPANIC
PERCENT HISPANIC OF DISTRICT POPULATION

20) FAM.INCOME
MEDIAN FAMILY INCOME OF DISTRICT

21) LEAD.LIMIT
Leadership term limits: Vote to limit the leadership terms of the speaker and committee chairmen to 8 years, Jan. 4, 1995.

22) NO PROXIES
Proxy Voting: Vote to ban proxy votes in any committee or subcommittee, Jan. 4, 1995

23) TAX UP 3/5
Tax Increases: Vote to require a three-fifths vote to raise taxes, Jan. 4, 1995

24) UNFUND.MAN
Unfunded Mandates: Vote to require Congress to provide cost estimates of regulatory mandates imposed upon state and local governments and to specify how the mandates are to be funded. Feb. 1, 1995.

25) UNF.MAN.2
Vote on requiring the "unfunded mandates" law to be reauthorized after 5 years, Feb. 1, 1995.

26) LINE VETO
Line Item Veto: Vote to give the president the line item veto, which would allow him to delete or reduce individual spending programs without rejecting entire appropriations bills, Feb. 6, 1995.

27) DEATH PEN1
Death Penalty: Vote to make enactment of the death penalty easier. The bill limits prisoners to one habeas corpus petition and requires that petitions be filed within two years for federal cases and one year for state cases, Feb. 8, 1995.

28) NAT.SECUR.
National Security Act: Vote on the National Security Act which limits the use of U.S. troops under United Nations command; reduces the U.S. contribution to U.N. peacekeeping operations; establishes a bipartisan commission on combat readiness, Feb. 16, 1995.

29) HLTH DEDUC
Health-insurance Deduction: Vote on extending a health-insurance tax break for self-employed Americans, Feb. 21, 1995.

30) MINOR.PREF
Minority Preferences: Vote on an attempt to keep the affirmative-action tax deferral for broadcasting, Feb.21, 1995.

31) DEFENSE SP
Defense Supplemental: Vote on giving an additional $3.2 billion to the Pentagon, Feb. 22, 1995.

32) RISK ASSES
Risk Assessment: Vote on a measure that would allow citizens to petition federal agencies for reviews of existing regulations, Feb. 28, 1995.

33) REG.OVER.
Regulatory Overhaul: Vote on incorporating four bills previously passed by the House (covering paperwork reduction, property rights, risk assessment and regulatory reform and relief) into one omnibus bill, March 3, 1995.

34) TAX CUT
Tax cut package: Vote on bill to give family tax credit, change the marriage penalty, expand retirement accounts, lower capital gains tax, and other tax changes, April 5, 1995.

35) PROD.LIAB.
Product Liability: Vote on bill to cap punitive damages in all civil cases at 3 times the amount of compensatory damages or $250,000 whichever is greater, March 10, 1995.

36) REG.MORAT
Regulatory Moratorium: Vote on bill to temporarily prohibit federal agencies from implementing new federal regulations, Feb. 24, 1995.

37) DEATH PEN2
Death Penalty Appeals: Vote on amendment to bar federal judges from extensively retrying state cases unless the decision was based on an arbitrary or unreasonable interpretation, Feb. 8, 1995.

38) EXCLUS.RUL
Exclusionary Rule: Vote on bill to allow prosecutors to use evidence obtained improperly, provided that the police believed that the search was legal, Feb. 8, 1995

39) PROP.RGTS1
Property Rights: Vote on a bill that would require the government to compensate landowners when federal regulations cause the value of any portion of their land to drop by 20 percent or more, March 3, 1995.

40) LEADER 103
HELD A LEADERSHIP POSITION IN HOUSE PRIOR TO THE 1994 ELECTION

41) % PAC $
PERCENT OF CAMPAIGN FUNDS RECEIVED FROM POLITICAL ACTION COMMITTEES (PACs)

42) $ PER VOTE
CAMPAIGN FUNDS SPENT PER VOTE RECEIVED

43) CAMPAIGN $
CAMPAIGN FUNDS RAISED FROM JAN. 1, 1993 to NOV. 28, 1994

44) % VOTE
Percent of vote received in the election

45) TERM LIMIT
Term Limits: Vote on a constitutional amendment to impose a 12-year lifetime limit on service in each chamber of Congress (March 29, 1995)

◆ LONG LABEL: NORC93 ◆

1) PRES IN 92
IF VOTED: DID YOU VOTE FOR CLINTON, BUSH OR PEROT?

2) PRES.88?
IF YOU VOTED IN 1988: DID YOU VOTE FOR DUKAKIS OR BUSH?

3) VOTE 92?
IN 1992, YOU REMEMBER THAT CLINTON RAN FOR PRESIDENT ON THE DEMOCRATIC TICKET AGAINST BUSH FOR THE REPUBLICANS AND PEROT AS AN INDEPENDENT. DO YOU REMEMBER FOR SURE WHETHER OR NOT YOU VOTED IN THAT ELECTION?

4) PARTY
GENERALLY SPEAKING, DO YOU USUALLY THINK OF YOURSELF AS A REPUBLICAN, DEMOCRAT, INDEPENDENT, OR WHAT?

5) LIB./CONS.
DOES RESPONDENT IDENTIFY AS A LIBERAL OR CONSERVATIVE?

6) SEX
RESPONDENT'S SEX

7) AGE
RESPONDENT'S AGE

8) RACE
RESPONDENT'S RACE (WHITE AND AFRICAN-AMERICAN ONLY)

9) MARITAL
ARE YOU CURRENTLY—MARRIED, WIDOWED, DIVORCED, SEPARATED, OR HAVE YOU NEVER BEEN MARRIED?

10) #CHILDREN
HOW MANY CHILDREN HAVE YOU EVER HAD? PLEASE COUNT ALL THAT WERE BORN ALIVE AT ANY TIME (INCLUDING ANY YOU HAD FROM A PREVIOUS MARRIAGE).

11) # SIBLINGS
HOW MANY BROTHERS AND SISTERS DID YOU HAVE? PLEASE COUNT THOSE BORN ALIVE, BUT NO LONGER LIVING, AS WELL AS THOSE ALIVE NOW. ALSO INCLUDE STEP-BROTHERS AND STEP-SISTERS, AND CHILDREN ADOPTED BY YOUR PARENTS.

12) RELIGION
RELIGIOUS PREFERENCE

13) CH.ATTEND
HOW OFTEN DO YOU ATTEND RELIGIOUS SERVICES?

14) SCH.PRAYER
THE UNITED STATES SUPREME COURT HAS RULED THAT NO STATE OR LOCAL GOVERNMENT MAY REQUIRE THE READING OF THE LORD'S PRAYER OR BIBLE VERSES IN PUBLIC SCHOOLS. WHAT ARE YOUR VIEWS ON THIS—DO YOU APPROVE OR DISAPPROVE OF THE COURT RULING?

Codebooks

15) VETERAN?
HAS RESPONDENT SERVED IN THE ARMED FORCES?

16) OCC. PREST
RESPONDENT'S OCCUPATIONAL PRESTIGE, APPROXIMATELY IN QUARTILES

17) EDUCATION
RESPONDENT'S EDUCATION (HS = HIGH SCHOOL)

18) FAMILY $
IN WHICH OF THESE GROUPS DID YOUR TOTAL FAMILY INCOME, FROM ALL SOURCES, FALL LAST YEAR, BEFORE TAXES THAT IS?

19) EVER UNEMP
AT ANY TIME DURING THE LAST TEN YEARS, HAVE YOU BEEN UNEMPLOYED AND LOOKING FOR WORK FOR AS LONG AS A MONTH?

20 UNIONIZED?
DO YOU (OR YOUR SPOUSE) BELONG TO A LABOR UNION?

21) HAPPY?
TAKEN ALL TOGETHER, HOW WOULD YOU SAY THINGS ARE THESE DAYS—WOULD YOU SAT THAT YOU ARE VERY HAPPY, PRETTY HAPPY, OR NOT TOO HAPPY?

22) DWELLING
DWELLING TYPE

23) REGION
REGION OF INTERVIEW

24) REG. AT 16
REGION OF RESPONDENT'S RESIDENCE WHEN AGE 16

25) PAR. BORN?
WERE BOTH YOUR PARENTS BORN IN THIS COUNTRY?

26) GUN OWNER?
DO YOU HAPPEN TO HAVE IN YOUR HOME (IF HOUSE: OR GARAGE) ANY GUNS OR REVOLVERS?

27) HUNTER?
DO YOU (OR DOES YOUR HUSBAND/WIFE) GO HUNTING?

28) READ PAPER
HOW OFTEN DO YOU READ THE NEWSPAPER—EVERY DAY, A FEW TIMES A WEEK, ONCE A WEEK, LESS THAN ONCE A WEEK, OR NEVER?

29) WATCH TV
ON THE AVERAGE DAY, ABOUT HOW MANY HOURS DO YOU PERSONALLY WATCH TELEVISION?

30) TV NEWS
TV—HOW OFTEN YOU WATCH TV NEWS SHOWS?

31) TV PBS
TV—HOW OFTEN YOU WATCH: PROGRAMS SHOWN ON PUBLIC TELEVISION. (TVPBS)

32) CAR RACES?
LAST 12 MONTHS DID YOU: GO TO AN AUTO, STOCK CAR, OR MOTORCYCLE RACE. (AUTORACE)

33) COUNTRY&W.
LIKE:COUNTRY AND WESTERN MUSIC

34) BIG BAND
LIKE: BIG BAND (SWING) MUSIC

35) CLASSICAL
LIKE:CLASSICAL MUSIC

36) POP/ROCK
LIKE:POP/ROCK MUSIC

37) RAP MUSIC
LIKE:RAP MUSIC

38) HEAVY METL
LIKE:HEAVY METAL MUSIC

39) WOMAN PREZ
IF YOUR PARTY NOMINATED A WOMAN FOR PRESIDENT, WOULD YOU VOTE FOR HER IF SHE WERE QUALIFIED FOR THE JOB?

40) MEN BETTER
MOST MEN ARE BETTER SUITED EMOTIONALLY FOR POLITICS THAN ARE MOST WOMEN.

41) SEGREGATE?
WHITE PEOPLE HAVE A RIGHT TO KEEP BLACKS OUT OF THEIR NEIGHBORHOODS IF THEY WANT TO, AND BLACKS SHOULD RESPECT THAT RIGHT.

42) FAIR HOUSE
SELECT FROM A. ONE LAW SAYS THAT A HOMEOWNER CAN DECIDE FOR HIMSELF WHOM TO SELL HIS HOUSE TO, EVEN IF HE PREFERS NOT TO SELL TO BLACKS OR; B. THE 2ND LAW SAYS THAT A HOMEOWNER CANNOT REFUSE TO SELL TO SOMEONE BECAUSE OF THEIR RACE OR COLOR

43) BUSING
IN GENERAL, DO YOU FAVOR OR OPPOSE THE BUSING OF BLACK AND WHITE SCHOOL CHILDREN FROM ONE DISTRICT TO ANOTHER?

44) BLACK PREZ
IF YOUR PARTY NOMINATED A BLACK FOR PRESIDENT, WOULD YOU VOTE FOR HIM IF HE WERE QUALIFIED FOR THE JOB?

45) ATH. SPEAK
SOMEBODY WHO IS AGAINST ALL CHURCHES AND RELIGION: IF SUCH A PERSON WANTED TO MAKE A SPEECH IN YOUR (CITY/TOWN/COMMUNITY) AGAINST CHURCHES AND RELIGION, SHOULD HE BE ALLOWED TO SPEAK, OR NOT?

46) COMMIE SPK
SUPPOSE THIS ADMITTED COMMUNIST WANTED TO MAKE A SPEECH IN YOUR COMMUNITY. SHOULD HE BE ALLOWED TO SPEAK, OR NOT?

47) RACIST SPK
IF SUCH A PERSON WANTED TO MAKE A SPEECH IN YOUR COMMUNITY CLAIMING THAT BLACKS ARE INFERIOR, SHOULD HE BE ALLOWED TO SPEAK, OR NOT?

48) FR. SPEECH
SCORE ON INDEX OF SUPPORT FOR FREEDOM OF SPEECH

49) TAX 2 HIGH
DO YOU CONSIDER THE AMOUNT OF FEDERAL INCOME TAX WHICH YOU HAVE TO PAY AS TOO HIGH, ABOUT RIGHT, OR TOO LOW?

50) EXECUTE?
DO YOU FAVOR OR OPPOSE THE DEATH PENALTY FOR PERSONS CONVICTED OF MURDER?

51) GUN CONTRL
WOULD YOU FAVOR OR OPPOSE A LAW WHICH WOULD REQUIRE A PERSON TO OBTAIN A POLICE PERMIT BEFORE HE OR SHE COULD BUY A GUN?

52) COURTS
IN GENERAL, DO YOU THINK THE COURTS IN THIS AREA DEAL TOO HARSHLY OR NOT HARSHLY ENOUGH WITH CRIMINALS?

53) WIRE TAP
EVERYTHING CONSIDERED, WOULD YOU SAY THAT, IN GENERAL, YOU APPROVE OR DISAPPROVE OF WIRETAPPING?

54) EX.BRANCH
CONFIDENCE? EXECUTIVE BRANCH OF THE FEDERAL GOVERNMENT.

55) LABOR?
CONFIDENCE IN: ORGANIZED LABOR.

56) PRESS?
CONFIDENCE IN: PRESS.

57) SCIENCE
CONFIDENCE? SCIENTIFIC COMMUNITY.

58) SUP.COURT
CONFIDENCE IN: U.S. SUPREME COURT.

59) CONGRESS?
CONFIDENCE IN: CONGRESS.

60) MILITARY?
CONFIDENCE IN: MILITARY.

61) BIG BIZ?
CONFIDENCE IN: MAJOR COMPANIES.

62) EDUCATIONC
CONFIDENCE IN: EDUCATION.

63) DEFECT
LEGAL ABORTION: IF THERE IS A STRONG CHANCE OF SERIOUS DEFECT IN THE BABY?

64) UNWANTED
LEGAL ABORTION: IF SHE IS MARRIED AND DOES NOT WANT ANY MORE CHILDREN?

65) MOM HEALTH
LEGAL ABORTION: IF THE WOMAN'S OWN HEALTH IS SERIOUSLY ENDANGERED BY THE PREGNANCY?

66) UNWED
LEGAL ABORTION: IF SHE IS NOT MARRIED AND DOES NOT WANT TO MARRY THE MAN?

67) ABORTION
LEGAL ABORTION: IF THE WOMAN WANTS IT FOR ANY REASON?

68) PORN.LAW?
CHOOSE: 1)THERE SHOULD BE LAWS AGAINST THE DISTRIBUTION OF PORNOGRAPHY WHATEVER THE AGE 2) THERE SHOULD BE LAWS AGAINST THE DISTRIBUTION OF PORNOGRAPHY TO PERSONS UNDER 18 3) THERE SHOULD BE NO LAWS FORBIDDING THE DISTRIBUTION OF PORNOGRAPHY.

69) SUIC.WISH
PERSON HAS THE RIGHT TO END OWN LIFE IF THIS PERSON IS TIRED OF LIVING AND READY TO DIE?

70) ANIM.RIGHT
ANIMALS SHOULD HAVE THE SAME MORAL RIGHTS THAT HUMAN BEINGS DO.

71) ANIM.TEST
IT IS RIGHT TO USE ANIMALS FOR MEDICAL TESTING IF IT MIGHT SAVE HUMAN LIVES.

72) GREEN TAX
AND HOW WILLING WOULD YOU BE TO PAY MUCH HIGHER TAXES IN ORDER TO PROTECT THE ENVIRONMENT?

73) GREEN CUT
AND HOW WILLING WOULD YOU BE TO ACCEPT CUTS IN YOUR STANDARD OF LIVING IN ORDER TO PROTECT THE ENVIRONMENT?

74) GREEN DIF
IT IS JUST TOO DIFFICULT FOR SOMEONE LIKE ME TO DO MUCH ABOUT THE ENVIRONMENT.

75) VEGGIE?
AND HOW OFTEN DO YOU REFUSE TO EAT MEAT FOR MORAL OR ENVIRONMENTAL REASONS?

76) US ACTIVE
DO YOU THINK IT WILL BE BEST FOR THE FUTURE OF THIS COUNTRY IF WE TAKE AN ACTIVE PART IN WORLD AFFAIRS, OR IF WE STAY OUT OF WORLD AFFAIRS?

77) OUT OF UN?
DO YOU THINK OUR GOVERNMENT SHOULD CONTINUE TO BELONG TO THE UNITED NATIONS OR SHOULD WE PULL OUT OF IT NOW?

78) FOREIGN $
SPENDING OR FOREIGN AID

79) DEFENSE $
SPENDING ON THE MILITARY, ARMAMENTS AND DEFENSE

80) WAR IN 10Y
DO YOU EXPECT THE UNITED STATES TO FIGHT IN ANOTHER WORLD WAR WITHIN THE NEXT TEN YEARS?

81) COMMUNISM
WHICH REPRESENTS VIEW OF COMMUNISM AS FORM OF GOVERNMENT: 1.WORST KIND OF ALL 2. BAD, BUT NO WORSE THAN SOME OTHERS 3. ALL RIGHT FOR SOME COUNTRIES 4. GOOD FORM OF GOVERNMENT

82) JAPAN
RATING: JAPAN

83) CANADA
RATING: CANADA

84) ISRAEL
RATING: ISRAEL

85) DEM/REP
PARTY PREFERENCE

86) CATH/PROT
DENOMINATION

87) OVER TAXED
DO YOU CONSIDER THE AMOUNT OF FEDERAL INCOME TAX WHICH YOU HAVE TO PAY AS TOO HIGH, ABOUT RIGHT, OR TOO LOW?

88) WELFARE $
WHAT ABOUT THE CURRENT LEVEL OF SPENDING ON WELFARE?

89) POOR $
WHAT ABOUT CURRENT LEVELS OF SPENDING ON ASSISTANCE TO THE POOR?

90) SOUTH/NOT
REGION OF INTERVIEW: SOUTH OR NON-SOUTH

91) COLLEGE/NT
RESPONDENT'S EDUCATION: ATTENDED COLLEGE OR NOT

92) OVER 50
RESPONDENT'S AGE: OVER OR UNDER 50

93) OVER 30
RESPONDENT'S AGE: OVER OR UNDER 30

◆ LONG LABEL: OLDHOUSE ◆

1) NAME
Representative's name

2) STATE
Representative's state

3) REGION
REGION

4) POSITION
NUMBER OF STATE POSITION

5) RACE/ETHNI
RACE OR ETHNICITY

6) WH/AF/HI
RACE AND/OR ETHNICITY

7) RELIGION
RELIGIOUS PREFERENCE

8) RELIGION 3
CATHOLIC, PROTESTANT OR JEWISH

9) PARTY
PARTY MEMBERSHIP

10) SOUTH DEM
PARTY WITH DEMOCRATS SEPARATED INTO SOUTHERN AND NON-SOUTHERN

11) AGE
AGE IN 1994

12) SEX
GENDER

13) LEADER
DOES MEMBER HOLD LEADERSHIP POSITION?

14) # TERMS
NUMBER OF TERMS SERVED IN THE HOUSE

15) ADA 1993
1993 VOTE RATING BY AMERICANS FOR DEMOCRATIC ACTION - A LIBERAL GROUP

16) CAMPAIGN $
AMOUNT OF CAMPAIGN MONEY RAISED FOR 1992 ELECTION

17) $ PER VOTE
CAMPAIGN SPENDING PER VOTE RECEIVED, 1992 ELECTION

18) % PAC $
PERCENT OF 1992 CAMPAIGN CONTRIBUTIONS RECEIVED FROM POLITICAL ACTION COMMITTEES (PACS)

◆ LONG LABEL: OLDSEN ◆

1) NAME
NAME OF SENATOR

2) STATE
SENATOR'S STATE

3) REGION
REGION

4) PARTY
POLITICAL PARTY

5) SOUTH DEM
PARTY BROKEN INTO SOUTHERN AND NON-SOUTHERN DEMOCRATS

6) SEX
SEX

7) RACE
RACE

8) EDUCATION
LEVEL OF EDUCATION

9) AGE
AGE

10) RELIGION
RELIGIOUS PREFERENCE

11) MARRIED
MARITAL STATUS

12) LAWYER
IS SENATOR A LAWYER?

13) VETERAN
HAS SENATOR SERVED IN THE ARMED FORCES?

14) TENURE
YEAR FIRST ELECTED, 1980 OR LATER, BEFORE 1980

15) % VOTE
PERCENT OF VOTE IN MOST RECENT GENERAL ELECTION, OVER OR UNDER 60%

16) CAMPAIGN $
TOTAL CAMPAIGN CONTRIBUTIONS IN MOST RECENT ELECTION, OVER OR UNDER $3 MILLION

17) $ PER VOTE
COST PER VOTE, OVER OR UNDER $6

18) % OUTSTATE
% OF CAMPAIGN FUNDS FROM OUT OF STATE, OVER OR UNDER 20%

19) % PAC $
% CAMPAIGN FUNDS RECEIVED FROM PACS

20) ADA 1993
RATING OF VOTING RECORD FOR 1993 BY AMERICANS FOR DEMOCRATIC ACTION, A LIBERAL LOBBYING GROUP (0 TO 100)   OVER OR UNDER 50

21) FAM.LEAVE
VOTE ON FAMILY LEAVE

22) HIV IMMIG.
BILL TO PERMIT IMMIGRATION BY PERSONS TESTING POSITIVE FOR HIV.

23) CLIN.BUDG
CLINTON BUDGET

24) GUN CONTRL
THE "BRADY BILL" REQUIRING A 5-DAY WAITING PERIOD TO PURCHASE A HANDGUN (PASSED)

25) NAFTA
THE NORTH AMERICAN FREE TRADE AGREEMENT, PASSED

◆ LONG LABEL: P1973-93 ◆

1) YEAR
YEAR OF SURVEY

2) RACE
RESPONDENT'S RACE

3) REGION
REGION OF INTERVIEW

4) AGE
RESPONDENT'S AGE GROUP

5) PARTY
GENERALLY SPEAKING, DO YOU USUALLY THINK OF YOURSELF AS A REPUBLICAN, DEMOCRAT, INDEPENDENT, OR WHAT?

6) ENVIRON $
SPENDING ON IMPROVING AND PROTECTING THE ENVIRONMENT

7) DEFENSE $
SPENDING ON THE MILITARY, ARMAMENTS AND DEFENSE

8) FOR. AID$
SPENDING ON FOREIGN AID

9) STAY IN UN
DO YOU THINK OUR GOVERNMENT SHOULD CONTINUE TO BELONG TO THE UNITED NATIONS OR SHOULD WE PULL OUT OF IT NOW?

10) ATH. SPEAK
SOMEBODY WHO IS AGAINST ALL CHURCHES AND RELIGION: IF SUCH A PERSON WANTED TO MAKE A SPEECH IN YOUR (CITY/TOWN/COMMUNITY) AGAINST CHURCHES AND RELIGION, SHOULD HE BE ALLOWED TO SPEAK, OR NOT?

11) COMMIE.SPK
SUPPOSE THIS ADMITTED COMMUNIST WANTED TO MAKE A SPEECH IN YOUR COMMUNITY. SHOULD HE BE ALLOWED TO SPEAK, OR NOT?

12) BIG BIZ?
CONFIDENCE? MAJOR COMPANIES.

13) EX.BRANCH
CONFIDENCE? EXECUTIVE BRANCH OF THE FEDERAL GOVERNMENT.

14) PRESS
CONFIDENCE? PRESS.

15) SCIENCE
CONFIDENCE? SCIENTIFIC COMMUNITY.

16) CONGRESS
CONFIDENCE? CONGRESS.

17) MILITARY
CONFIDENCE? MILITARY.

18) INTERMARRY
DO YOU THINK THERE SHOULD BE LAWS AGAINST MARRIAGES BETWEEN BLACKS AND WHITES?

19) FAIR HOUSE
SELECT FROM A. ONE LAW SAYS THAT A HOMEOWNER CAN DECIDE FOR HIMSELF WHOM TO SELL HIS HOUSE TO, EVEN IF HE PREFERS NOT TO SELL TO BLACKS; OR B. THE 2ND LAW SAYS THAT A HOMEOWNER CANNOT REFUSE TO SELL TO SOMEONE BECAUSE OF THEIR RACE OR COLOR.

20) GUN CONTRL
WOULD YOU FAVOR OR OPPOSE A LAW WHICH WOULD REQUIRE A PERSON TO OBTAIN A POLICE PERMIT BEFORE HE OR SHE COULD BUY A GUN?

21) EXECUTE
DO YOU FAVOR OR OPPOSE THE DEATH PENALTY FOR PERSONS CONVICTED OF MURDER?

◆ LONG LABEL: SENATE ◆

1) NAME
SENATOR'S NAME

2) STATE
SENATOR'S STATE

3) REGION
REGION

4) PARTY
POLITICAL PARTY

5) SOUTH DEM.
PARTY: SOUTHERN & NORTHERN DEMOCRATS AND REPUBLICANS

6) SEX
SEX

7) RACE/ETH
RACE OR ETHNICITY

8) AGE
AGE

9) RELIGION
RELIGIOUS PREFERENCE

10) EDUCATION
LEVEL OF EDUCATION

11) MARITAL
MARITAL STATUS

12) LAWYER?
IS SENATOR A LAWYER?

13) NEWCOMER?
NEW AND HOLDOVER SENATORS

14) REELECT96?
SENATOR IS UP FOR RE-ELECTION IN 1996

15) ACCOUNTBLE
Congressional Accountability: Federal laws, including the Civil Rights and the Americans with Disabilities Act, shall be applicable to Congress, Jan. 11, 1995

16) PAY CUTS
Congressional Pay Cuts: Vote to table an amendment to the Congressional Accountability Act that would have reduced lawmakers' pay if they didn't meet budget limits on spending, Jan. 11, 1995.

17) UNFUND.MAN
Unfunded Mandates: If Congress passes a bill imposing costs of more than $50 million on state and local government, it must specify how the measure will be financed, Jan. 27, 1995.

18) BAL.BUDG.
Balanced Budget: Vote on constitutional amendment to balance the federal budget by 2002, March, 1995 (Dole is coded as a "yes" although he actually voted no to allow the bill to be re-introduced. If the majority leader votes for a bill introduced by the majority party and the bill is defeated, it may not be re-introduced.)

19) LINE VETO
Line Item Veto: Vote on bill to provide for the separate enrollment of each individual spending item in an appropriation bill, targeted tax breaks in a revenue bill or new entitlement spending so that the president may veto each item, March 23, 1995.

20) RELIGION 3
RELIGIOUS PREFERENCE

21) %PAC $
PERCENT OF CAMPAIGN FUNDS RECEIVED FROM POLITICAL ACTION COMMITTEES (PACs)

22) $ PER VOTE
COST PER VOTE RECEIVED FOR MOST RECENT ELECTION

23) CAMPAIGN $
TOTAL CAMPAIGN FUNDS RAISED

License Agreement

READ THIS LICENSE AGREEMENT CAREFULLY BEFORE OPENING THE DISKETTE PACKAGE. BY OPENING THIS PACKAGE YOU ACCEPT THE TERMS OF THIS AGREEMENT. *MicroCase*® Corporation, hereinafter called the Licensor, grants the purchaser of this software, hereinafter called the Licensee, the right to use and reproduce the following software: **American Government:** *An Introduction Using MicroCase* in accordance with the following terms and conditions.

Permitted Uses

- You may use this software only for educational purposes.
- You may use the software on any compatible computer, provided the software is used on only one computer and by one user at a time.
- You may make a backup copy of the diskette(s).

Prohibited Uses

- You may not use this software for any purposes other than educational purposes.
- You may not make copies of the documentation or program disk, except backup copies as described above.
- You may not distribute, rent, sub-license or lease the software or documentation.
- You may not alter, modify, or adapt the software or documentation, including, but not limited to, translating, decompiling, disassembling, or creating derivative works.
- You may not use the software on a network, file server, or virtual disk.

THIS AGREEMENT IS EFFECTIVE UNTIL TERMINATED. IT WILL TERMINATE IF LICENSEE FAILS TO COMPLY WITH ANY TERM OR CONDITION OF THIS AGREEMENT. LICENSEE MAY TERMINATE IT AT ANY OTHER TIME BY DESTROYING THE SOFTWARE TOGETHER WITH ALL COPIES. IF THIS AGREEMENT IS TERMINATED BY LICENSOR, LICENSEE AGREES EITHER TO DESTROY OR RETURN THE ORIGINAL AND ALL EXISTING COPIES OF THE SOFTWARE TO THE LICENSOR WITHIN FIVE (5) DAYS AFTER RECEIVING NOTICE OF TERMINATION FROM THE LICENSOR.

MicroCase Corporation retains all rights not expressly granted in this License Agreement. Nothing in the License Agreement constitutes a waiver of MicroCase Corporation's rights under the U.S. copyright laws or any other Federal or State Law.

Should you have any questions concerning this Agreement, you may contact MicroCase Corporation by writing to: MicroCase Corporation, 1301 120th Avenue N.E., Bellevue, WA 98005, ATTN: College Publishing Division.